Sound Phonics

Teacher's Guide

Carol Matchett

Schofield & Sims

The activities in this **Teacher's Guide** are supported by materials in the **Teacher's Resource Book**, indicated by the symbol ▭.

Further resources are available as free downloads from the Schofield & Sims website (www.schofieldandsims.co.uk), and are indicated by the symbol ⊡. These materials are updated as necessary to meet the requirements of the National Curriculum.

First published in 2014

Copyright © Schofield & Sims Limited 2014

Author: Carol Matchett
Carol Matchett has asserted her moral right under the Copyright, Designs and Patents Act, 1988, to be identified as the author of this work.

British Library Catalogue in Publication Data:
A catalogue record for this book is available from the British Library.

Commissioning by **Carolyn Richardson Publishing Services** *(www.publiserve.co.uk)*
Design by **Oxford Designers & Illustrators**
Printed in the UK by **Page Bros (Norwich) Limited**

ISBN 978 07217 1223 9

Contents

Introduction

Scope and sequence chart

Teaching notes

Sound Phonics Phase One   1

Sound Phonics Phase Two   9

Sound Phonics Phase Three Book 1   19

Sound Phonics Phase Three Book 2   31

Sound Phonics Phase Four   39

Sound Phonics Phase Five Book 1   48

Sound Phonics Phase Five Book 2   56

Sound Phonics Phase Five Book 3   65

Sound Phonics Phase Six Book 1   71

Sound Phonics Phase Six Book 2   79

Assessment in Sound Phonics   87

Spelling choices and guidelines   91

Glossary   95

Introduction

Sound Phonics

Sound Phonics supports the teaching and learning of phonics. It builds knowledge systematically, moving incrementally from simple to more complex aspects of phonics work, developing the skills and knowledge needed to read and spell words.

The series follows the same basic structure as the phonics resource *Letters and Sounds* (© Crown copyright 2007) and includes the following components.

- This **Teacher's Guide** helps you, the teacher, parent or other adult helper, to teach phonics. It provides guidance on introducing key skills and knowledge, using the activity books and consolidating learning. Opportunities for the children to practise phonic skills and apply phonic knowledge are suggested.

- The **Teacher's Resource Book** contains photocopiable resources for use in the activities outlined in this Guide. **General resources** are suitable for several Phases, while **Activity book resources** relate to specific books.

- **Rhymes for Reading** is a photocopiable collection of phonically decodable rhymes with accompanying **Teaching notes**, aimed at Phases Two to Four. These provide a valuable opportunity to apply phonic knowledge in a real reading context at an early level.

- The **activity books** are carefully graded and contain exercises to practise the phonic knowledge and skills introduced through teaching. The first book is a reusable stimulus book, while the remaining nine are one-per-child activity books. Clear teaching objectives are summarised at the foot of each page.

Note: the activity books, resource book and photocopiable rhymes may be used to support other incremental phonics programmes.

Using Sound Phonics

Sound Phonics is based on the teaching model 'teach → practise → apply → assess', as described below.

Teach

The **Teaching notes** in this Guide explain how each learning focus can be introduced to a group or class of children, using interactive and multi-sensory activities. The learning focus is kept clear in short, direct sessions and the **Teacher's Resource Book** provides materials to use in the activities.

Practise

The **Sound Phonics** activity books provide practice material to consolidate new learning. The activities are most effective if completed in a small group, with an adult present, as this allows the children to make and listen to sounds, and to practise their phonic skills orally. The children should ask an adult to check their work so that any difficulties can be addressed immediately.

Further practice activities are described in this Guide and supported by material in the **Teacher's Resource Book**.

Apply

From **Sound Phonics Phase Two**, the activity book exercises require the children to apply their phonic knowledge and skills to read decodable captions, sentences and questions, moving towards complete texts in Phase Six. In the **Teacher's Resource Book** you will find word swap activities and sentences for reading and writing practice.

Rhymes for Reading provides phonically decodable rhymes for Phases Two to Four, as well as **Teaching notes** to help you use the rhymes effectively in the learning environment. The rhymes allow the children to apply their new phonic knowledge in a real reading context at an early stage.

This **Teacher's Guide** features 'Applying phonics' boxes, which recommend ways to apply phonic knowledge and skills in other areas of learning.

Assess

Each page in the activity books has a clear teaching objective, summarised in the 'Focus' notes, which helps to guide on-going assessment. In addition, assessment tasks and statements are provided in the activity books, and record and analysis sheets can be found in the **Teacher's Resource Book**.

Full details on carrying out assessments, analysing results and using the record sheets are given on pages 87–90 of this Guide.

Sound Phonics Teacher's Guide

The **Sound Phonics Teacher's Guide** helps you to use all the **Sound Phonics** materials effectively. It includes **Teaching notes** on how to introduce and revise the key learning points in each Phase, and provides clear references to relevant material in other books in the series.

The **Teaching notes** allow you to plan your phonics teaching around the exercises in the **Sound Phonics** activity books, and suggest suitable introductory and extension activities for each learning focus. These frequently require resources provided in the **Sound Phonics Teacher's Resource Book**, which are indicated by the symbol ⊡. Further resources are available as free downloads from the Schofield & Sims website (www.schofieldandsims.co.uk), and are indicated by the symbol ⊡.

The **Teacher's Guide** features teaching suggestions and guidance for each **Sound Phonics** activity book. The contents panel at the start of each set of notes will help you to find a suitable activity for your lesson.

The **Teaching notes** include:

● an outline of the learning focus

● activities to introduce and teach each learning focus to a class or group, such as introducing a letter and sound, or demonstrating segmenting for spelling

● ideas to facilitate effective use of the workbook activities, including strategies for helping those children who have difficulty with a particular activity

● extension activities to follow on from the **Sound Phonics** activities, providing further practice and consolidating new knowledge

● ways to help the children to apply their new knowledge and skills, both in phonics sessions and in other areas of the curriculum.

Scope and sequence chart

	2. Phase Two	3. Phase Three Book 1	4. Phase Three Book 2
Practice of new graphemes	Letter Sets 1–5 (**s, a, t, p, i, n, m, d, g, o, c, k, e, u, r, h, b, f, l**)	Letter Sets 6–7 (**j, v, w, x, y, z, zz, qu**) plus **sh, ch, th, ng** and **ll, ss, ff, ck**; letter names introduced	**ai, ee, igh, oa, oo, ar, or, ur, ow, oi, ear, air, er**
Revision of graphemes	Letter Sets 1–4	Letter Sets 1–5	Letter Sets 4–7 plus consonant digraphs
Reading activities	Blending for reading CVC words with letters from Sets 1–5; tricky words; captions; sentences; signs; notes	Blending for reading CVC words with new graphemes; two-part words, tricky words; sentences; clues; questions; captions	Blending for reading words with vowel digraphs; two-part words; tricky words; questions; sentences; clues; captions
Spelling and writing activities	Segmenting for spelling (oral segmenting of CVC words; recall of letters needed)	Segmenting CVC words for spelling (selecting letters/graphemes needed)	Segmenting for spelling
Letter formation	Pointing and finger tracing only	Occasional tracing over dotted letters, with arrows indicating direction	Tracing over dotted letters, with arrows indicating direction – and copying them
Assessment areas	1. Letter sounds (Sets 1–5) 2. Blending; segmenting (oral and for reading/spelling) 3. Tricky words	1. Sounds (Sets 1–7 plus consonant digraphs) 2. Blending; segmenting 3. High-frequency words 4. Tracing letters	1. Sounds (Phase Two and Three graphemes) 2. Blending; segmenting 3. Letter formation 4. Tricky words

	5. Phase Four	6. Phase Five Book 1	7. Phase Five Book 2
Practice of new graphemes	Consolidation only	**ay**, **ou**, **ie**, **ea**, **oy**, **ir**, **aw**, **ue**, **ew**, **oe**, **au**, **ey**, **a-e**, **e-e**, **i-e**, **o-e**, **u-e**, **wh**, **ph**	Alternative pronunciation of known graphemes
Revision of graphemes	Letter Sets 1–7, Phase Three graphemes	Phase Three graphemes	Graphemes from Phases Two, Three and Five
Reading activities	Blending for reading words with adjacent consonants; two-part words; tricky and high-frequency words; sentences; questions; clues; captions	Reading words with up to two parts; words with split graphemes; new graphemes; tricky and high-frequency words; speech; questions	Reading words with alternative pronunciations; words with up to two parts; tricky and high-frequency words; questions; sentences; clues; stories; homographs
Spelling and writing activities	Segmenting to spell words with adjacent consonants; spelling tricky words	Spelling words with two parts; words with new and split graphemes; writing captions; completing sentences with tricky words	Spelling words with two parts; tricky words; question words; writing sentences and captions; answering questions
Letter formation	Tracing over dotted letters with no arrows – and copying them; writing most letters independently	Tracing over some dotted words; writing letters and words independently, forming letters correctly	Tracing over some dotted words; writing letters and words independently, forming letters correctly
Assessment areas	1. Sounds 2. Blending; segmenting 3. Letter formation 4. Tricky words	1. Sounds 2. Blending; segmenting 3. Letter formation 4. Tricky words	1. Sounds (including alternative pronunciations) 2. Blending; segmenting 3. Tricky words

	8. Phase Five Book 3	9. Phase Six Book 1	10. Phase Six Book 2
Practice of new graphemes	Alternative spelling of known phonemes	Less common grapheme–phoneme correspondences	Less common grapheme–phoneme correspondences
Revision of graphemes	Recognition of graphemes; alternative pronunciations and spellings	Long and short vowel sounds; alternative pronunciations (Phase Five)	Grapheme check Phases Three and Five; suffixes **s** and **es**
Reading activities	Reading words with up to two parts; words with new graphemes; tricky words; speech bubbles; sentences	Reading activity instructions; words with up to three parts; tricky words; words with less common graphemes; stories	Reading activity instructions; words with up to three parts; tricky words; words with less common graphemes; story titles; poems; stories; proofreading a story
Spelling and writing activities	Choosing from alternative spellings; selecting correct spelling of phonemes; spelling two-part words and long vowel sounds; completing and writing sentences with tricky words	Choosing from alternative spellings; making correct spelling choices; spelling two-part, longer and tricky words; writing sentences and captions; adding suffixes	Choosing from alternative spellings; spelling tricky words; proofreading a story; spelling two- and three-part words; spelling high-frequency and topic words; writing sentences; adding prefixes and suffixes
Letter formation	Tracing over some dotted words; writing words and sentences independently, with each letter formed correctly	Writing words and sentences independently; forming letters correctly	Writing words and sentences independently; forming letters correctly
Assessment areas	1. Sounds (Phase Five) 2. Blending; segmenting 3. High-frequency words	1. Reading aloud (accuracy and fluency) 2. Spelling words; segmenting; adding suffixes 3. Reading and spelling high-frequency words	1. Reading aloud (accuracy and fluency) 2. Spelling words; segmenting; adding suffixes 3. Reading and spelling high-frequency words

Teaching notes

Sound Phonics Phase One

1 Sound discrimination	
2 Rhythm	
3 Rhyme	
4 Alliteration	
5 Oral blending and segmenting	

Sound Phonics Phase One differs from the other books in this series, as the children do not need to write on the page to complete the activities. Instead, the reusable stimulus book sets out a progression of phonics and pre-phonics activities for an adult to carry out with a child or a small group of children. The activities encourage the children to listen carefully, identify sounds and appreciate rhythm, rhyme and **alliteration**. Some letter sounds are introduced, as well as oral **segmenting** and **blending**. This helps to form a strong foundation for the systematic phonics teaching that begins in Phase Two.

Each activity is described in the Phase One activity book and a clear learning objective is given at the foot of each page. This guides you in observing the children and assessing their knowledge, skills and understanding.

In the **Teaching notes** for Phase One you will find 'Observe and record' suggestions to focus your observations during the activities. Significant achievements and difficulties can be recorded on the *Group activity sheet* (▢). This information can then be summarised on the Phase One *Record sheet* (▢).

Note: there are no formal assessment tasks in Phase One, as the 'Observe and record' process is used throughout.

The focused activities described in **Sound Phonics Phase One** should be embedded in a language-rich, engaging and experience-based learning environment. The **Teaching notes** suggest ways of using play activities, structured games, book sharing, outdoor and indoor environments and everyday activities to introduce and develop early phonic skills. Talk should be a central part of all activities at this stage, as language development is essential for future progress in reading and writing.

1a Sound discrimination: environmental sounds

Before children can begin a structured phonics programme they need to be good listeners. They should be able to distinguish between sounds and understand how to make and control sounds.

Introductory activities

● Encourage the children to be good listeners, pointing out and praising good listening. Model good listening by being quiet, following the source of a sound with your eyes, or using a gesture (such as putting a hand to your ear) to indicate listening.

● Go on 'listening walks' or 'listening adventures' in different settings and have 'listening moments' at different times of day. Extend the children's vocabulary by talking about sounds and what makes them. Help the children to explore and make sounds in various settings, perhaps splashing in puddles, crunching through dry leaves or tapping a stick on a fence.

● Introduce sound-making in play activities, talking about sounds and the things that produce them. You could discuss animal sounds while playing with a model farm, or vehicle sounds while playing with a toy garage.

● Make sounds during role play or in the home corner, for example, *'Ping' – oh, that's the microwave!* Encourage the children to make sounds associated with the setting. Discuss the sounds and introduce appropriate vocabulary.

● Add environmental sounds to stories, such as *boing* for a bouncing ball or *eeek* for an opening door. Encourage the children to join in or to make the sounds when rereading or retelling a story.

● Create a 'sound box' and fill it with items that make different noises. These could include a bell, a bag of marbles, a squeaky toy or some tissue paper. Let the children explore the contents. Talk about the sounds and ask the children to imitate them. When they are familiar with the contents, encourage the children to guess a hidden object from its sound, or ask one child to imitate a sound while the others guess which object it is.

Observe and record: note how well each child imitates sounds and recalls, identifies and distinguishes between familiar sounds.

Sound Phonics activities (pages 4–6)

● The children should listen for and discuss the sounds they might hear in different environments.

● Talk with the children about animals and imitate the sounds that they make. Sing 'Old Macdonald had a farm', imitating the animal sounds.

● The children talk about sounds made by the familiar items given. They should be able to recall the sounds and distinguish between them.

● Ask the children to talk about sounds that they like and dislike.

1b Sound discrimination: instrumental and body percussion sounds

Introductory activities

● Set up a music- or sound-making area with a range of instruments. Allow the children to explore the instruments freely. Join in the activity, encouraging the children to find ways to play the instruments loudly and quietly or quickly and slowly. Talk about the different sounds made, for example, *I shake it – it makes a long sound; I tap it – it makes a short sound.* Take the instruments outside to see if the sounds are different.

● Use the instruments in structured games to encourage careful listening, perhaps playing an instrument hidden from view and asking the children to identify it. Alternatively, tell them to perform an action each time you play a particular instrument, for example, *Stand up if you hear the triangle 'ting'.*

● Provide materials for the children to make their own instruments in the sound-making area, including simple shakers with different contents and drums made from containers. Talk about the sounds produced. Play the instruments in a 'pots and pans band' marching round the playground.

● Use instruments, sound effects and actions in familiar rhymes or songs, such as a sound and action for each verse of 'The wheels on the bus'. You could also choose instruments to represent different characters or animals in a story. Put instruments and sound-making objects in story sacks and sound boxes.

● Look for opportunities in the day to discuss body percussion sounds. Try rubbing hands after coming in from the cold, stamping feet in the hall or playground, tapping fingers on a tabletop to sound like rain, or making sounds with your lips to accompany drawing ond 'writing'.

● Use body percussion sounds to enhance a story, for example, blowing through your lips for the sound of the wind. Encourage the children to join in (or suggest ideas) and to do the same when they re-enact stories.

● Play *Follow the sound leader*. Make a sound or a simple sound pattern on an instrument and then pass the instrument round the group for everyone to copy the sound or pattern. This also works with body percussion (for example, *stamp, stamp, clap, clap*).

> **Observe and record:** note how well each child makes and copies sounds. Does the child talk about sounds using appropriate vocabulary (*loud*, *quiet*, *long*, *short*)?

Sound Phonics activities (pages 7–8)

● The children say the rhyme 'Humpty Dumpty sat on a wall', making vocal sounds to add to the ends of the lines. Encourage the children to join in with the sounds and use actions to go with the rhyme.

● Talk with the children about body percussion sounds and discuss the characteristics of the different sounds given. Demonstrate the sounds for the children and encourage them to copy you.

2   Rhythm

Songs and rhymes are important because they help children to tune into the rhythm and sound of the English language. The children will need plenty of informal activities to develop their awareness of rhythm and rhyme.

Introductory activities

● Make 'rhyme time' a daily activity by singing and chanting rhymes. Repeat old favourites and regularly introduce new rhymes so that the children build up a good repertoire of rhymes and songs.

● Encourage the children to join in with action rhymes and songs such as 'Teddy bear, teddy bear' or 'Two fat gentlemen', so that the words become familiar. To encourage careful listening and articulation, introduce actions to go with particular words or phrases.

● Use opportunities to sing or chant a rhyme appropriate to an everyday activity, such as 'Miss Polly had a dolly' in role play, or 'This is the way we wash our hands' when getting ready for lunch.

● Use outdoor and indoor spaces to help the children to respond to rhythm. Encourage them to move appropriately, for example, skipping or marching to the beat of 'If you're happy and you know it' in the playground, or rocking to 'Row, row, row your boat' when seated on the carpet.

● As rhymes become familiar, try increasing or decreasing the speed for each verse. Add sound effects or substitute other words that fit the rhythm, such as '10 red apples hanging on the tree'.

Observe and record: notice how well each child joins in the activity. Observe how clearly the child says the words and moves to the beat. Look for contrasts in speed and volume.

Sound Phonics activities (pages 9–12)

● Chant or sing the rhymes, using movements and actions to fit the words.

● Make up your own verses to traditional rhymes, and encourage the children to offer suggestions of their own.

● If some of the children have difficulty joining in with the rhymes, coordinating actions with the words or moving to the rhythm, try slowing the pace of delivery so that the words are clearer. This also gives the children more time to prepare for joining in.

3 Rhyme

The ability to recognise rhyme and suggest rhyming words will help the children to read and spell words in the future. In Phase One they develop an awareness of rhyme, how it sounds and how it feels to say rhyming words. This will help them to recognise when two words rhyme (and when they do not).

Introductory activities

● Regularly include rhymes in book sharing sessions. Use changes of intonation and expression to emphasise the rhyming words and encourage the children to join in with rhymes and repeated patterns.

● In 'rhyme time' say a familiar rhyme, pausing before the final word so that the children provide the rhyming word. Make a deliberate mistake, such as saying a word that doesn't rhyme, and see if the children correct you. Invent new verses and rhymes based on old favourites, for example, 'The farmer's in his den' could become 'The mouse is in his house'.

● Point out rhyme when it occurs naturally, for example, *Jack, put it back –* *'Jack' and 'back' rhyme!*

● Incorporate rhyme into other activities. Make up rhymes when playing with puppets or toys. Say a rhyming couplet and let the children guess the rhyming word, for example, *The little green frog / He sat on a l … log.*

● Collect objects with names that rhyme and put them in a container, such as a box or basket. Reveal and name each object in turn, then put them back in the container. Say, *Do they sound the same? Let's play the rhyming game.* Pick out two items that rhyme, say their names and then add, *That rhymes!* For example, *A book and a hook – that rhymes!* Repeat with other pairs, encouraging the children to join in with, *That rhymes!* Include some pairs of non-rhyming objects, for example, *A cat and a bell – that doesn't rhyme.*

● Vary this activity. Pass the container round the group and ask each child to find a pair of objects that rhyme, or give one object to a child and ask him or her to find its rhyming partner. On another occasion take out three objects, two that rhyme and one that does not. Ask the children to identify the odd one out.

> **Observe and record:** notice how well each child recognises words that rhyme, distinguishes between rhyming and non-rhyming words, and suggests a word to rhyme with a given word.

Sound Phonics activities (pages 13–18)

- If the children have difficulty recognising rhyme, say the words slowly, emphasising the rhyming sound at the end. Continue to practise the introductory activities.

- The children join in with rhyming games, recognising rhyming pairs and suggesting appropriate words to complete a rhyme.

- On page 18, they should identify the object with a name that does not rhyme with the others.

Extension activities

Games to practise rhyme

Rhyming pairs: place the rhyming pairs *picture cards* (▢) face down on the table. The children should take it in turns to pick up two cards and name the objects. If the names rhyme, the child keeps the cards. If they do not, the cards are returned and the next child has a go.

Pass the rhyme on: pick up an object, such as a hat. Slowly count to three and then name the object (*1 ... 2 ... 3 ... hat*). On the word, *hat*, pass the object to a child and continue the slow count (*1 ... 2 ... 3 ...*). The child should add a rhyming word and pass the object to the next child. Continue round the group, with the children adding rhyming words after the count of three. Allow nonsense and repeated words as long as they rhyme.

Rhyme tennis: say a word and ask a child to respond with a word that rhymes.

I-spy: say, *I spy with my little eye something that rhymes with ...*

Note: not all children will be able to generate a series of rhyming words in Phase One, so these activities could also be used as the children begin to learn letters and sounds in Phase Two.

---

4 Alliteration

Developing a sense of alliteration helps the children to tune into the sounds at the start of words. This is essential for identifying initial **phonemes** and for recognising the different letter sounds.

Introductory activities

- Use stories, rhymes, songs, poems and tongue twisters to develop a sense of alliteration. 'Ring a ring of roses', 'Fee fi fo fum', 'Ten tired tigers' and 'Bob the Builder™' all work well. Emphasise the initial sound and encourage the children to say them with you. Comment on the alliteration, for example, '*Ten tired tigers*' – *can you hear the t sound at the start of all those words?*

- Use the children's names to focus on initial sounds. Make up alliterative phrases, such as *Sam sit slowly on the seat* or *Tara tap the tabletop*. Play *I-spy* using the children's names or use initial sounds when lining up, for example, *Line up if your name starts with sss*.

- Use alliteration to name characters, toys, puppets or pets (see pages 11–13 and 20–21 of this Guide), or use the *character downloads* (⬇). Emphasise the initial sounds and let the children say the names. See if they can suggest ideas.

- Incorporate alliteration into play and everyday activities. For example, in outdoor play, you might have **b**ats, **b**ouncy **b**alls and **b**ean **b**ags one day and **h**ula **h**oops, **h**oopla and **h**opping another. In role play, you could go shopping for items whose names start with a particular sound, such as **c**akes, **c**auliflower and **c**andles.

- Collect two sets of objects, each set with objects that have the same initial phoneme. Place all the items in a lucky dip box or hide them in the sandpit. Ask a child to pull out one object at a time, name it and place it in one of two hoops so that the objects are grouped by initial sound. Each time an object is added to a hoop, say together the names of all the objects in that group, emphasising the initial sound (for example, *cup, car, coin*).

- Repeat this activity with different sets of objects to introduce new sounds. Keep each set of objects in its own box. Once you have several boxes, put out a different box every few days for the children to explore. Invite the children to take out the objects and name them, emphasising the initial sound. See if they can suggest other objects to go in the box.

Observe and record: note how well each child says the sounds, responds to alliteration, identifies initial sounds in words and discriminates between initial sounds.

Sound Phonics activities (pages 19–25)

- The children join in with tongue twisters and alliterative sentences.

- They should identify and sort objects by their initial sounds, and think of more words that begin with the same sound.

- If the children have difficulty articulating sounds clearly, ask them to copy you, saying a word and emphasising the initial sound, for example, *mmmap*. Show the children how to make the sounds into the mirror so that they can see how the lips and tongue move.

Extension activities

Games to practise alliteration

Alliterative pairs: place the initial sound *picture cards* (▭) face down on the table. The children should take it in turns to turn over two cards and say the names of the objects. If they begin with the same sound, the child keeps the pair. If they do not, the cards are returned.

Odd one out: display four pictures of items, three that begin with the same sound and one that does not. Ask the children to identify the odd one out.

Although letters are not formally introduced until Phase Two, some children will show an awareness of them and the sounds they represent. To encourage this, add *grapheme cards* (▭) and plastic letters to the sound boxes or hold up a grapheme card when you play alliteration games. This will help the children to associate letters with their sounds. Draw attention to letter shapes at the start of words, both in the learning environment and in books.

5   Oral blending and segmenting

Being able to hear separate phonemes in words is a key phonic skill, essential for good progress in reading and spelling. The children need experience of oral blending and segmenting before they move on to the structured phonics programme in Phase Two.

Introductory activities: blending

● Introduce oral blending in everyday activities. Give the children instructions, segmenting and blending the sounds in the final word, for example, *Let's fill the **p-o-t** pot*. Occasionally do this with the final word of a rhyme.

● Use a toy robot or the *Tog posting box* (▭) in a focused activity to introduce **sound talk**. Ask the robot his name and tell the children that he says, ***T-o-g***. Say, ***T-o-g,** Tog*, and ask the children to repeat this. Ask Tog other questions, such as *What's your favourite sandwich? (**j-a-m**, jam) What's your favourite colour? (**r-e-d**, red)* Always say the answer in sound talk and then say the whole word. Ask the children to repeat this on each occasion. As the children become familiar with the concept of blending sounds, see if they begin to say the blended word before you, after hearing the sound talk.

● Set up a treasure hunt, maybe hiding 'gold coins' around the room. Explain that Tog has left some clues about where he has hidden his treasure, but part of the clue is in sound talk. Ask the children to help you. Read a clue, saying the last word in sound talk, for example, *It is by the **b-e-ll** or It is under the **m-a-t***. See if the children put the sounds together and say the word. If they do not, repeat the sound talk and say the word, then ask the children to repeat the whole sentence.

---

*Note: while some sounds can be sustained (**s, f, m**) others should be short (**c, b, d**). Pronounce sounds in a way that makes blending easy and particularly avoid adding 'uh' (rather than **buh**, say **b**).*

> **Observe and record:** focus on how well each child blends sounds and recognises whole words.

Sound Phonics activities (pages 26–28)

● Demonstrate oral blending and sound talk to introduce these processes.

● Introduce Tog the robot and explain that he speaks in sound talk (see introductory activities). Encourage the children to blend Tog's sound talk to make words.

● Play *I-spy* again, but this time say the words in sound talk.

Extension activities

● Display a selection of objects that represent simple **CVC words**, or select suitable *picture cards* from the **Teacher's Resource Book**. Say the name of an object in sound talk and see if the children can say the word and identify the object. They can then post the object in the *Tog posting box* (▭).

Introductory activities: segmenting

● Use Tog the robot to introduce oral segmenting (the reverse of oral blending). Invite the children to tell Tog the name of objects in sound talk. Model this process, for example, *Tog says, 'What's this?' Let's tell him it's a hat. Hat **h-a-t***. Ask the children to repeat the sound talk to Tog.

● Continue this activity with other objects. See if the children can segment a word for themselves and praise them for 'speaking sound talk'. Be aware that while some children will do this easily, others will need more practice.

● Include Tog in a range of contexts and activities to facilitate the use of sound talk. For example, you might name items for Tog when playing with a toy farm (such as *pig* or *dog*) or the children could give Tog a secret message.

Observe and record: notice how well the children segment words into phonemes.

Sound Phonics activities (pages 29–30)

● Demonstrate oral segmenting, breaking words up into sound talk. Ask the children to repeat the sentence.

● Ask the children to choose an object and to say its name using sound talk.

● Continue to model the process for any children who find segmenting difficult, but always ask them to repeat the sound talk after you.

Extension activities

● The children who can segment and blend sounds could play games using *picture cards* (▭). Give each child the same set of cards. One child selects a picture and says it in sound talk, without showing the card. The partner then blends and says the word, before finding the picture in his or her set of cards.

Sound Phonics Phase Two

1 Introducing the letter

2 Writing the letter

3 Revising the letter

4 Blending for reading

5 Segmenting for spelling

6 Reading sentences with tricky words

The **Sound Phonics** activity books for Phases Two to Six are one-per-child activity books. Successful completion of an activity indicates a child's progress towards the learning focus at the foot of the page. 'Observe and record' suggestions are no longer provided, as the activity books provide a written record of each child's progression. Evidence from completed exercises and observation of activities should be used to check that the children have grasped the intended learning focus. Record anything that needs to be revisited or reinforced and cover this again in a later session. Problems and misunderstandings should not be ignored.

At the back of each **Sound Phonics** activity book for Phases Two to Six, you will find a set of assessment tasks and statements. These are designed to help you to monitor each child's acquisition of key knowledge and skills. Full details on these assessments are provided on pages 87–90 of this Guide.

In **Sound Phonics Phase Two**, the children are introduced to 19 letters and sounds, and begin to **blend** and **segment** words using these letters.

1 Introducing the letter

Introduce each letter in a multi-sensory way, so that the children hear and speak the sound, and see the letter alongside pictures and objects that recall the sound. Provide opportunities to feel the shape of the letter and to practise the movements required to form it. The activities below can be adapted for each letter using the suggestions on pages 11–13 and 20–21 of this Guide.

You will need: *grapheme card (▭); corresponding plastic letter; objects beginning with the letter or sound; 'Sid the snake' toy character or download (▽).*

Introductory activities

● Display the grapheme card. Say some names or words starting with the sound, for example, *Sssarah*, *Sssam*, *sssand*. Ask the children to repeat them after you. Say the **sss** sound and ask the children to repeat it.

● Show the objects and say the words with the children. Ask them to give the thumbs up if the object name begins with the focus sound, and thumbs down if it doesn't.

● Introduce a toy character or *character download* such as 'Sid the snake'. If you are using a toy, give it a badge with the letter **s**. Say the character's name, exaggerating the **s** sound, and ask the children to repeat it. Say an alliterative sentence, such as *Sssid the sssnake ssslithers in the sssun*. Ask the children to say it with you.

● Point to the picture on the grapheme card and say the word, exaggerating the sound. Point to the letter on the grapheme card and say the letter sound. Trace the letter shape with your finger ('finger write') and say the sound again. Ask the children to copy you, saying the sound and tracing the shape in the air.

● Point to the letter on the toy's badge or on the download and say the sound **s**. Again, ask the children to say the sound and trace the shape in the air.

● Hold up the character and the grapheme card a number of times. If you hold up the character, the children should say the name. If you show the grapheme card, they should say the letter sound and trace the letter shape in the air.

Sound Phonics activities (pages 4–9, 11–12, 15–16, 19–20, 25, 27–28, 33–34, 37–38)

● In pairs, the children practise saying the letter sound and identifying items that begin with the sound. Support the children by saying the names of the items, exaggerating the initial sound.

Extension activities

● Hold the character, saying its name and the letter sound, for example, *Sid the snake – s*. Point to the letter on the badge or download as you say, **s**. Pass the character round the group, asking the children to hold it and say its name and the letter sound. Notice how clearly each child articulates the sound.

● Use plastic or wooden letters to reinforce the letter. Give the children opportunities to touch and explore the shapes. Ask them to put all the **s** shapes on a **s**aucer (or **e** into **e**gg cups, **b** into a **b**ucket, **h** into a **h**at).

● Reinforce the letter shape and sound in other contexts. You could make a **s**ock **s**nake and form it into the letter **s**, curly **c** out of clay, **g** out of **g**lue and **g**old **g**litter or **d** out of **d**ough. The focus of these activities should always be to link the letter shape to its sound.

● Put the character and grapheme card on a tray. Ask the children to add to the tray any items (or pictures of items) that begin with the letter sound.

● Give the children copies of the grapheme card to put near objects in the classroom beginning with the sound. Continue this activity in other areas of the learning environment, perhaps with **b**ean **b**ags, **b**alls and **b**ats in outdoor play, or **p**ens, **p**aints and **p**ots in the art area.

● Stick the grapheme card on the front of a 'zigzag book', made from a concertina of paper. Ask the children to draw pictures starting with the letter sound on each page.

● Encourage the children to look for initial letters in shared reading and everyday contexts, perhaps on name cards, trays or labels in the classroom.

2 Writing the letter

Letter formation should also be introduced at this stage, so that the movements for making each letter are linked to its sound and shape. Although some children will not yet have the dexterity to write all the letter shapes, they should experience forming the letters in the air, in sand or on chalkboards, practising the basic 'down, up and round' movements. Other children will be able to write most of the letters in pencil with the correct formation.

....

You will need: *grapheme card* (▭).

....

Introductory activities

● Display the grapheme card. Place your finger on the dot and trace the letter shape several times on the card. Alternate between saying the sound and a letter formation patter, such as, *Over his head, slide down the snake* for **s**. Ask the children to copy, using their finger to write in the air. Further writing patter suggestions can be found on pages 11–13 and 20–21 of this Guide.

● The children should then trace the letter shape with their finger on the carpet or table in front of them, and then on their own hand. Repeat the patter as they do this.

Sound Phonics activities (pages 4–9, 11–12, 15–16, 19–20, 25, 27–28, 33–34, 37–38)

● Ask the children to run their finger over the letter shape at the top of the page in **Sound Phonics Phase Two** and to join in with the patter.

● If appropriate, ask the children to write the letter on the green panel, between the letter shapes, as you say the patter. Those children with good pencil control can also write the letter next to the pictures beginning with that sound.

Extension activities

● Provide a range of writing materials so that the children can freely practise letter formation. Children who do not have the physical maturity to write the letters should practise the basic 'down, up and round' movements using small whiteboards, sand trays, chalkboards and paints.

● As before, link the materials to the letter sound, practising **s** in **s**and, **p** in **p**aint, **i** with **i**nk pens or **g** in **g**old pen.

● Set up a writing table by covering a tabletop completely with paper, and provide a range of writing materials so that the children can write letters all over it. Encourage them to say the patter or the letter sound as they write.

Multi-sensory ideas for introducing letters and sounds

Note: a downloadable character (☑) is available for each of the alliterative sentences below. These can be printed and used in activities or displays.

Letter	Alliterative sentence	Character and objects	Writing patter
s	Sid the snake slithers slowly in the sun.	Sid the snake (sock, saucer, stars, spoon, sandal, samosa, soup, salt)	*Over his head, slide down the snake.*
a	Al the alligator had an apple.	Al the alligator (apple, arrow, ant, ambulance, alphabet, axe, alarm)	*Over the apple, round and down.*
t	Tug tiger Tess by the tail.	Tiger Tess (tin, twig, tie, toast, towel, tortoise, tape, tyre, torch)	*Down the tiger's tail, pencil off, stripe across.*

Letter	Alliterative sentence	Character and objects	Writing patter
p	Pat Percy panda on the paw.	Percy panda (purse, pen, peg, pig, paints, pizza, pebble)	*Down, up to the top and round the panda's head.*
i	Dip in Izzy's invisible ink.	Izzy's incredible invisible ink (ink, insect, invitation, igloo)	*Down, pencil off, ink dot on top.*
n	No, no, not in Nicky's nest!	Nicky the nightingale (nut, nail, net, notebook, necklace, naan, noodles)	*Down, up and over we go.*
m	"Mmm," says Mimi mouse.	Mimi mouse (mug, mirror, milk, mouse, mints, mask, map, monster)	*Do a **n** and make it **m**.*
d	Donna dog digs in the dirt – dig, dig, dig.	Donna dog (doll, dice, dish, dog, duck, doughnut, dummy)	*All the way round, up to the top, down and flick the dog's tail.*
g	Gabby the gorilla gets a good g-g-goal.	Gabby the gorilla (goat, glove, glue, grapes, grass, guitar, gold, gate)	*Go all the way round, go down and hook in the goal.*
o	Ollie the octopus goes on, off, on, off.	Ollie the octopus (orange, omelette, ostrich, olives, otter)	*Over the octopus and all the way round.*
c	Can Curtis cat cut a cake?	Curtis cat (car, cup, cap, candle, carrot, comb, comic, card, cactus)	*Over the cake, curl round.*
k	Kick, kick, kick goes Kiki the kangaroo.	Kiki the kangaroo (kettle, kennel, key, kite, koala, kitten, kiwi)	*All the way down, pencil off, a kick and flick.*
e	Ed the elephant puts his egg in the e-e-egg cup.	Ed the elephant (envelope, egg, elf, engine)	*Across, over the top of the egg and round.*
u	Uncle Ugg holds his umbrella upside down.	Uncle Ugg (umbrella)	*Down, under the umbrella, up and down.*
r	Rachel rabbit races red rockets.	Rachel rabbit (robot, rock, rocket, radio, ribbon, rope, rice, racket, rag)	*Down, up, over and off.*
h	Hopping Holly holds her hula-hoop	Hopping Holly (hat, hoop, horse, hook, honey, hen, house, hose, hay, hammer)	*All the way down, half way up and over.*
b	B-b-b goes Bobbie's bouncing ball.	Bobbie bear (bus, balloon, book, brick, banana, badge, ball, butter)	*All the way down, bounce back up and round.*

Letter	Alliterative sentence	Character and objects	Writing patter
f	Fergus frog found flowers by the fence.	Fergus frog (flag, frog, fork, fan, felts, fudge, flower, fox, fish, fairy)	*Over and down the fork, strike through.*
l	Leo lion likes lemon and lime.	Leo lion (lolly, lorry, leaf, letter, lemon, lime, lamp, lock, lipstick)	*From the top – all the way down the ladder.*

*Note: as in Phase One, pronounce sounds in a way that makes blending easy. While some sounds can be sustained (**s, f, m**) others should be short (**c, b, d**) so avoid adding 'uh' sounds (rather than **buh**, say **b**).*

3 Revising the letter

After a letter has been introduced, the children need to practise recognising and recalling it. Revision activities appear regularly in **Sound Phonics Phase Two**, but it is a good idea to start every phonics session with a quick 'warm-up' based on previously learnt letters and sounds.

You will need: *grapheme cards for known letters (▢); plastic letters; a letter frieze or Phase Two and Three sound mat (▢).*

Introductory activities

● Hold up each grapheme card in turn and ask the children to say the letter sound. If necessary, use the picture to help them. Repeat until the children respond quickly and automatically to each letter.

● Display a letter frieze or the *Phase Two and Three sound mat*. Ask the children to say the sounds as you point to the letters at random. Increase the speed to encourage automatic letter recognition.

● Write the letters on the board one at a time and ask the children to say each letter sound. This time there is no picture clue, so use the grapheme card or *Phase Two and Three sound mat* to recap the sound if necessary. Again, increase the speed to encourage a quick response.

Sound Phonics activities (pages 13, 21, 31)

● Point to each letter at random and ask the children to say the letter sound. Aim for automatic recognition, but allow a little thinking time to begin with. Use the grapheme cards or *Phase Two and Three sound mat* to recap if necessary. Record any letters that are not recognised and include them in future 'warm-up' sessions.

● Reverse the process. Say a letter sound and ask the children to point to the letter.

● When working without an adult, the children can practise this in pairs. One child points to a letter on the page and the other says the sound.

Extension activities

● Organise the children into pairs or small groups and place a set of grapheme cards face down in front of each group. Ask the children to take it in turns to turn over the cards and say the letter sound. If a child says the sound immediately, he or she wins the card. If not, it goes to the bottom of the pile.

● Play a similar game with plastic letters in a bag. The children pull out a letter and say the sound, keeping the letter if they say it correctly.

● Introduce the *Stepping stones* game (☐) towards the end of Phase Two. Try playing the game on a larger scale in the classroom, using big dice and hoops with the letters written on them. The children should throw the dice and jump along the 'stepping stones', saying the sound of the letters they land on. If a child makes a mistake, he or she returns to the start.

*Note: grapheme cards and the **Stepping stones** game can also be taken home for additional practice.*

4   Blending for reading

Once the children are comfortable with the first six letters and sounds, they can learn how to say and blend these sounds to read words. Blending for reading activities are found throughout the Phase Two activity book.

. . . .
You will need: *sound button words* (☐); *Tog posting box* (☐).
. . . .

Introductory activity

● Put all the *sound button words* in a bag. Take out a word and display or write it on the board, for example, *tin*. **Sound talk** the word, touching the **sound buttons**, then say the word, for example, *t-i-n tin*. Say the sound talk and ask the children to say the word. Repeat with a second word.

● Take out a third word. Ask the children to sound it with you, pressing the sound buttons and then saying the word. Repeat with one or two words, making sure that the children blend the sounds to make the word.

● Let the children sound and blend a word from the bag. If they find this difficult, repeat the process together. Repeat with another word. You could ask the children to say the word to a partner first, so that they all have a chance to blend the word. This also allows you to check individual children.

Sound Phonics activities (pages 10, 14, 17, 22, 26, 29, 35, 39)

● The children should sound, blend and read words, either matching them to pictures or deciding whether they are real or made up. The children should then reread the words with a partner to check their answers. Repeated reading will help the children to recognise words automatically.

● If a child has difficulty with this activity, pay attention as he or she sounds and blends the words. If the child has difficulty saying the letter sounds, more practice is needed at letter recognition. Note any problematic letters and include them in letter recognition practice.

● If the child has difficulty blending the sounds, he or she may be saying the sounds too slowly or may need further practice at oral blending. Repeat the sounds so that the child can blend them, or model the process and ask the child to repeat after you. Some children will need a lot of practice before they fully grasp blending.

Extension activities

● Use the *sound button words* in games such as *Pairs, Count on it* or *In the pot* for further practice at blending to read words (see below).

● Compile a set of word cards to use in a scavenger hunt, for example, *tin, map, pot* and *dog*. The children should then read the words and find an object in the classroom to represent each word.

● Use the *blank word cards* (▭) to add some made-up words to the selection of word cards. Ask the children to read and sort the words, putting the real words in the *Tog posting box*.

Games to practise blending for reading

Pairs: in pairs, give each child the same set of *word cards* (▭). One child picks a card, then blends and reads the word aloud. The partner should then find the word in his or her word cards. The children check that they each have the same word, and make a pair. When all the words are in pairs, the children should ask an adult to check their answers.

Count on it: give four word cards to each child. Say a word and ask the children to see if it is written on any of their cards. If so, they should put a counter on the card. Check the cards, removing any incorrectly placed counters, and continue. The first child with counters on all their cards wins.

In the pot: put all the word cards in a pot and use the *blank word cards* (▭) to add some cards with *pot* written on them. The children each take out a word in turn. If they read the word correctly, they may keep it – if not, it goes back in the pot. If a child pulls out a '*pot*' card, his or her cards must all go back in the pot.

Feed Tog: this requires word cards that fall into two categories, for example, words with and without a particular sound, or real and made-up words. In pairs, the children read the words and decide whether they fit the criteria. If they do, the children put the word cards into the *Tog posting box*. Older children may sort them onto a *word sort* sheet (▭).

Against the clock: the children start with their word cards face down. Using a timer, see how many words the children can sound, blend and read before the time runs out. If a child recognises a word instantly, there is no need to sound it first.

Applying phonics to reading

Children need plenty of opportunities to apply their phonic knowledge in a range of contexts, so that they can begin to understand the purpose of their phonic learning. Demonstrate blending to read words regularly and in a range of contexts, and encourage the children to use their new skills in both formal and informal reading activities.

Reading in the classroom

Use the classroom environment and activities in different areas of learning to provide opportunities for reading. Display **decodable** signs in the classroom, such as *Put pens in the pot*, and add decodable captions to displays of work or photos, for example, *The sun is hot*; *Jen has a pet cat*.

Read the signs with the children to demonstrate blending words in a real reading context. When there is enough decodable print in the classroom, the children can go on 'reading walks' to read signs and captions. Do this with a group of children first. When they are familiar with the activity they can go on reading walks in pairs, as an independent activity.

Reading decodable texts

As early as possible, the children should begin reading short books and simple texts such as poems or instructions. Such reading material should be appropriate to the children's reading abilities, so that they can apply their skills and knowledge successfully.

In **Rhymes for Reading**, you will find some rhymes suitable for the end of Phase Two. Enlarge a rhyme to read with a group of children, so you can demonstrate reading words in context. Alternatively, use individual copies for guided or one-to-one reading. Before reading, remind the children of their new skills and knowledge, and prompt them to use this as they read the rhyme. Once they have read the text, the children will benefit from rereading the rhyme. This will improve their fluency and increase their familiarity with many words.

A range of reading experiences

Not all the reading material you use will be decodable at this stage. Many books will be chosen for their content and language, and for pure enjoyment. Shared reading sessions will often focus on book knowledge and comprehension. However, even in these shared sessions you can still find opportunities to reinforce the children's phonic learning. You might ask the children to sound and blend one or two words containing known letters. When sharing a book for enjoyment, you could sound some of the words in the title, for example, *B-o-b Bob and the big d-o-g dog – Bob and the big dog*. You could also write a decodable sentence or caption to slip into a familiar book or to put in a story sack for the children to read.

5   Segmenting for spelling

Segmenting for spelling is also introduced in Phase Two. It is the reverse process of **blending** and requires the children to orally segment sounds and recall letters. Children generally need a lot of practice before they fully grasp segmenting for spelling.

. . . .
You will need: *three-box phoneme frame* (▢); *phoneme frame letters* (▢); *a toy robot or the Tog posting box* (▢).
. . . .

Introductory activity

● Show Tog the robot to the children. Remind the children that Tog only speaks in sound talk and ask them to sound Tog's name. Say some words and ask the children to say them in sound talk like Tog, for example, *top t-o-p* and *cap c-a-p*. Some children may find it helpful to make a chopping action as they segment each word.

- Display the *three-box phoneme frame* and the appropriate set of *phoneme frame letters*. Say a **CVC word** and ask the children to say the word in sound talk like Tog. Demonstrate finding each letter in turn and fitting it into the frame. Sound talk the letters in the frame and say the word.

- Repeat with a few words. Involve the children in segmenting the words and finding the letters to put in the phoneme frame.

Sound Phonics activities (pages 18, 24, 30, 40)

- The children should sound the words and select the letter needed to complete the phoneme frames. Many children will find this activity easier if they first use *phoneme frame letters* to build the words on a phoneme frame.

Extension activities

- Ask the children to use the phoneme frame and letters to make a word featured in the **Sound Phonics** activities. Demonstrate swapping a letter to make another word, perhaps changing *dot* to *dog*. Sound the new word and choose another letter to change. Repeat to make more new words.

- Choose another CVC word which has a new meaning when the final consonant is changed, such as *mud*. Write the first two letters on the phoneme frame. Ask the children to guess the word and to put the last letter on the phoneme frame.

- The table below provides a list of words that can be made with each set of *phoneme frame letters* in the **Teacher's Resource Book**.

Sets 1–3	Sets 1–4	Sets 1–5
dig, dip, dog, dot, gap, gas, God, got, pad, pat, pig, pit, pod, pot, sad, sag, sat, sip, sit, tag, tap, tip, Tog, top	den, dug, get, gum, gun, Meg, men, met, mud, mug, net, nut, red, rug, rum, run, rut, Ted, ten, tug, tum	beg, Ben, bet, bug, bun, but, get, gun, leg, let, rub, rug, run, rut, tub, tug

6 Reading sentences with tricky words

As soon as the children start to blend words, introduce them to reading simple captions. This is the first step towards reading books and other complete texts. They will need to learn some **high-frequency words** with unusual or unfamiliar **graphemes**. These are referred to as **tricky words**. Five tricky words are introduced in **Sound Phonics Phase Two**, as well as *and*.

You will need: *reading sentence* or *caption with the tricky word* (▢); *words to swap* (▢).

Introductory activities

- Display or write the tricky word sentence on the board. Read it, pointing to each word. Use sound talk to read one or two of the decodable words, for example, *S-i-d Sid in the m-u-d mud – Sid in the mud*. Ask the children to join in if they can, or otherwise to repeat it after you.

- Explain that some words have tricky letters. Read the caption again, pointing to each word, and then point to the tricky word, for example, *the*. Say this word.

- Write the word on the board. Sound talk it and discuss the 'tricky bit' (the part that does not represent the expected sound). Read the word a few times and then read the whole caption again.

- Change one or two words in the caption but keep the tricky word, for example, *Ben in the den*. Read the new caption together. Use sound talk to read the new words but not the tricky word.

Sound Phonics activities (pages 23, 32, 36, 41–43)

- The children read the captions and sentences, matching them to a picture.

- They should read the captions with a partner, and then an adult, to check whether they have matched the pictures correctly. Rereading helps the children to become familiar with other high-frequency words as well as the tricky word, so that they can recognise them automatically.

Extension activities

- Give the children a caption or sentence from the **Teacher's Resource Book** to read. Cut it up into separate words and ask the children to rebuild it. They should then read the sentence to a partner, to check whether it makes sense.

- Cut out the set of *words to swap* (⬜) and use them to make a new caption. Ask the children to read the new caption with their partner and see if it makes sense.

- The children swap words to make new captions or sentences to read with their partner. They should then choose a caption to stick down on paper and illustrate.

- Refer to the tricky word throughout the day, and in shared reading, so that the children learn to recognise it.

- Use the tricky word in classroom signs, notices and captions for the children to read. You could base these on phrases read in the introductory session.

Sound Phonics Phase Three Book 1

1 Introducing the letter

2 Writing the letter

3 Revising the letter

4 Word endings **ff**, **ll**, **ss**, **ck**

5 Letter names

6 Graphemes **sh**, **ch**, **th**, **ng**

7 Blending for reading

8 Segmenting for spelling

9 Reading sentences

10 Reading words with two parts

In Phase Three Book 1, the children encounter the remaining seven letters and sounds, plus the double consonants **ff**, **ll**, **ss**, **ck** and the four consonant **digraphs ch**, **sh**, **th**, **ng**. They are also introduced to the letter names.

---

*Note: the **ks** and **kw** sounds that represent the letters **x** and **q** both comprise two phonemes. As the children do not need to be taught this, **ks** and **kw** are treated as single phonemes in blending and segmenting activities.*

---

1 Introducing the letter

· ·

You will need: *grapheme card (▭); corresponding plastic letter; character toy or download (▽); and objects beginning with the letter.*

· ·

Introductory activities

● Display the grapheme card. Say the sound three times, then a name or word starting with that sound, such as *j-j-j-jam, j-j-j-Joe*. Continue the chant and ask the children to join in. Hold up an object as you say the sound and let the children say the word. Ask the children to suggest further suitable words.

● Introduce a character for the letter and sound, such as Jack and Jill dolls or character downloads. If you are using toys, give the characters a **j** letter badge. Say the characters' names in an alliterative sentence, for example, *Jack and Jill jump in juicy j-j-j-jelly*. Ask the children to repeat it.

● Show the grapheme card. Point to the picture and say the name of the object, exaggerating the sound. Point to the letter and say the sound again. Point to the letter on the badge or download and ask the children to say the sound.

● On the grapheme card, move your finger over the letter shape and say the sound. Ask the children to copy you, tracing the shape in the air or on the carpet or table. Repeat several times, saying the sound and tracing the letter.

● Explain that if you hold up the character or object, the children should say the word, and if you hold up the grapheme card, they should say the sound. Do this a number of times.

● To adapt these activities for other Phase Three letters, see the table on pages 20–21 of this Guide.

Sound Phonics activities (pages 11–14, 18–20)

● The children practise saying the letter sound and should then identify the objects beginning with that sound.

● Notice how well each child recognises the letter and enunciates the sound.

Extension activities

● Put the character and grapheme card on a tray. Ask the children to select and place on the tray objects beginning with the letter.

- Make copies of the grapheme card for the children to place next to any objects in the classroom that begin with the sound.

- Make 'zigzag books' by folding a long strip of paper into a concertina. The children can then draw in items that start with the new letter sound.

- Organise a letter search. Ask the children to look for the new letter in shared reading and in everyday reading contexts.

- Ask the children to sort through a collection of plastic letters. Give the children a task, such as putting all the **j** shapes in a **j**am **j**ar, the **v** shapes in a **v**ase, or the **x** shapes in a bo**x**.

- Use play activities that link the sound and letter, perhaps dressing up as **w**itches and **w**izards and making **w**ands with **w** on them.

2 Writing the letter

In Phase Three Book 1, the children practise correct letter formation by tracing over the letter shapes in pencil. Introduce the formation of each new letter as you introduce the letter sound and practise letter recognition.

. . . .

You will need: *grapheme card* (📖).

. . . .

- Display the grapheme card. Trace the shape of the letter on the card, starting at the dot. Do this a number of times, saying the sound and the letter formation patter. Ask the children to copy you, using their finger to write in the air. Repeat and ask the children to trace ('finger write') the letter, first on the carpet or table in front of them and then on their hand.

- Ask the children to run their finger over the letter shape at the top of the appropriate page in **Sound Phonics Phase Three Book 1** and to join in with the patter. Then ask them to write the letter on the pink panel, between the letter shapes. Children with good pencil control can also write the letter next to the pictures beginning with the sound.

- Provide the children with a range of writing materials with which to practise forming the letter. You could also use letter formation practice to reinforce the sound, perhaps writing **y** in **y**ellow paint, **w** in **w**hite chalk, **j** in **j**am, or even **qu** with a **qu**ill.

- Write the letters in contexts that reinforce the sounds, such as a string of **zzz** coming from a bee or a sleeping person.

Multi-sensory ideas for introducing letters and sounds

Note: a downloadable character (👤) is available for each of the alliterative sentences below. These can be printed and used in activities or displays.

Letter	Alliterative sentence	Character and objects	Writing patter
j	Jack and Jill jump in juicy j-j-jelly.	Jack and Jill (jam, jar, jigsaw, jelly, juice, jug, jet, jacket, joke, jumper, jeans)	*Down, under the line, hook, pencil off, and dot the top.*

Letter	Alliterative sentence	Character and objects	Writing patter
v	Vicky the v-v-van delivers veg in the valley.	Vicky the van (van, vase, vest, velvet, vacuum, varnish, vinegar, voucher)	*Down the valley and up the other side.*
w	Wild winds waft Wendy the witch.	Wendy the witch (watch, worm, windmill, wood, wig, wax, wafer, web, wand)	*Down and up and down and up.*
x	Rex the fox will fix the box.	Rex the fox (box, fox, six)	*Slope one way – cross back.*
y	Young Yasmin has a y-y-yoyo.	Young Yasmin (yacht, yogurt, yellow, yolk, yoyo)	*Down, under, up, all the way down and hook.*
z	Zelda the zebra can zip and zoom.	Zelda the zebra (zip, zebra, zoo, zodiac)	*Across, zigzag down and across.*
qu*	Quackers the duck gives a quick 'quack-quack'.	Quackers the duck (quill, quiz, quavers, quilt, queen, quince)	*Over the top, all the way round, down under the line, a quick flick.*

*Note: Explain that **q** always needs **u** after it in the English language, although the **u** is never spoken.*

3 Revising the letter

Automatic recognition of letters is important when **blending** for reading, and being able to recall letters associated with sounds is essential when **segmenting** for spelling. Continue to provide regular opportunities to practise recognition, recall and formation of Phase Two and Three letters and sounds. It is a good idea to start every phonics session with a quick 'warm-up' based on previously learnt letters and sounds.

• •
You will need: *grapheme cards for known letters (▢); the Stepping stones game (▢); counters; Phase Two and Three sound mat (▢).*
• •

Introductory activities

● Hold up each grapheme card in turn and ask the children to say the letter sound as quickly as they can. If necessary, use the picture to help them.

● Write the letters on the board one at a time. Ask the children to say the letter sound as soon as the letter is complete. Increase the speed so that the children have to respond more quickly.

● Say a sound and ask one of the children to point to the corresponding letter on the board. Ask the child to trace over the letter shape as you say the patter. The rest of the children should join in with the patter and trace the letter on the carpet or table in front of them.

Sound Phonics activities (pages 4, 22)

● Point to the **graphemes** at random and ask the children to say the sound. Encourage quick responses but allow thinking time if required. Use the *sound mat* to recap any letters that the children do not recognise. Make a note of these, so that they can be included in future 'warm-up' sessions.

● Say a letter sound and ask the children to find and write over the letter. Make sure that they form the letter correctly. If necessary, support them by saying the letter formation patter as they write. The children can practise this in pairs, with one child pointing and the other saying the sounds.

Note: the children can write over the letters several times in different colours.

Extension activities

● For additional practice at letter recognition, use a set of grapheme cards or plastic letters in pair or small group games (see page 15 of this Guide).

● Use the *Stepping stones* game (📖) to practise letter recognition. Increase the challenge by asking the children to say the letter sound and then name an item starting (or ending) with that sound.

● Those who need more practice at letter formation can practise writing the letters, using the page in the activity book or the *Letters* and *Lines* handwriting downloads (📎) to help them.

4   Word endings ff, ll, ss, ck

The double consonants above (and **zz**) are often found at the end of short words. In Phase Three Book 1, the children learn that these 'double letters' represent the same sound as each letter separately. This helps to introduce the idea that two letters can sometimes represent one sound.

• •

You will need: *sound button words* (📖).

• •

Introductory activities

● Display a sound button word, such as *hiss*, *tell* or *pick*. Point to or draw the **sound buttons**, then sound and say the word, for example, *t-e-ll tell*. Explain that a long sound button goes under the double letter to show that it represents one sound. When the children see a double letter at the end of a word, they should say just one sound. Run your finger under the double letter and ask the children to say the sound. Ask the children to sound and blend the word.

● Display two or three more words and ask the children to **sound talk** and read them, touching the sound buttons.

Sound Phonics activities (pages 7, 8)

● The children read words with double letter endings and match them to the pictures.

● Make sure that the children touch the sound buttons as they say the sounds. Remind the children to move their finger along the long sound button as they say the sound at the end of each word.

Extension activities

● Use *sound button words* in games such as *Pairs*, *Count on it* and *In the pot* (page 15 of this Guide).

5 Letter names

· ·

You will need: *'The alphabet song' and 'The cheerleaders' abc' (Sound Phonics Phase Three Book 1, pages 24 and 35); an alphabet frieze;* **grapheme cards** (▭); *the Stepping stones game* (▭); *counters.*

· ·

Introductory activities

● Teach the 'The alphabet song' and 'The cheerleaders' abc' over a period of time before formally introducing the letter names.

● Show a grapheme card, such as **m**. Explain that every letter in the alphabet has a name and a sound. Point to the letter, and tell the children its name and the sound that it represents. Repeat with other grapheme cards.

● Display the alphabet frieze and ask the children to sing 'The alphabet song' or 'The cheerleaders' abc'. Point to the letters as they are named in the song. Continue to practise this over a number of days.

Sound Phonics activities (pages 24, 35)

● In pairs, the children practise pointing to the letters on the page as they sing or chant their names.

Extension activities

● Play the *Stepping stones* game. This time, ask the children to say the letter name rather than its sound.

● Read the rhyme 'It is an odd thing' in **Sound Phonics Rhymes for Reading**.

6 Graphemes sh, ch, th, ng

Once all 26 letters have been introduced, the children begin to learn some two-letter graphemes that represent other sounds. In Phase Three Book 1, they encounter the four consonant digraphs, **sh, ch, th, ng**.

---

*Note: the **th** grapheme represents two slightly different sounds, a 'whispery' unvoiced sound (**th**in) and a 'buzzing' voiced sound (**th**en). However, the difference is not great and the children will usually switch easily to the appropriate sound when reading. As a result no distinction is made between the two sounds in **Letters and Sounds** and **Sound Phonics**.*

· ·

You will need: *grapheme card* (▭); *voting paddles* (▭).

· ·

Introductory activity

● Say the sound, for example, **sh**. Where appropriate, make up an action to go with it, such as fingers to lips for *ssh*. Encourage the children to join in with the sound and action.

● Say words or names starting or ending with the grapheme, exaggerating the sound, for example, **ss**hop, fi**ss**h or **Ss**harif. Encourage the children to join in, repeating words and offering suggestions.

● Introduce a toy character or *character download* (▱) to reinforce the sound and say an alliterative sentence (see page 25 of this Guide). Ask the children to repeat it.

● Display the grapheme card. Explain that this sound needs two letters that the children already know. Run your finger along the long sound button and say the sound. Remind the children that the long sound button shows that the two letters represent one sound. Point to the grapheme on the character's badge or on the download and ask the children to say the sound.

● Write the new grapheme (**sh**) on the *voting paddles*. Hold one up and ask the children to say the sound. Give out the *voting paddles*. Ask the children to run their finger over and under the letters, saying the sound.

● Write a list of words on the board and ask the children to hold up their *voting paddle* when they see a word with **sh**. Invite a child to draw a long sound button under the two-letter grapheme.

Note: see pages 11–13 and 20–21 of this Guide for ways to introduce graphemes and sounds.

Sound Phonics activities (pages 25–26, 31–32)

● In pairs, the children should practise saying the sound and identifying words that begin or end with it.

● Support the children by saying the names of the items, exaggerating the focus sound.

Extension activities

● Ask the children to collect items that begin or end with the focus sound. They could also place grapheme cards next to suitable items in the classroom. Give the activity an appropriate name, such as *Champion's* ***ch****allenge*, or *Think of a **th*** (with the winner sitting on a **th**rone).

● Make 'zigzag books' by folding a long strip of paper into a concertina. You could then add pictures of items whose names start or end with the sound.

● Use the *voting paddles* throughout the day in different contexts to reinforce the grapheme and its sound. For example, hold up the **sh** paddle to ask for quiet, hold up **ch** paddles and form a train that goes **ch**-**ch**-**ch** round the playground, or say and give the 'thumbs up', if the **th** paddle is held up.

● Use activities in other areas of learning to reinforce the grapheme and its sound. You could make **ch**ocolate **ch**ip cookies to **ch**ew, or dazzli**ng** ri**ng**s fit for a ki**ng**. Alternatively, explore the sounds made by bells – which go *di**ng** dong*, and which go *ti**ng**-a-li**ng**?

Multi-sensory ideas for introducing letters and sounds

Note: a downloadable character (⬚) is available for each of the alliterative sentences below. These can be printed and used in activities or displays.

Grapheme	Alliterative sentence	Character and objects	Action
sh	Shy Shane the sheep shouts, "Ssh!"	Shane the sheep (shell, shoe, ship, shark, shorts, shawl, shield, shirt)	*Ssh with fingers to lips.*
ch	Charlie the cheeky chick goes cheep, cheep, cheep.	Charlie the cheeky chick (chalk, cheese, cherry, chick, chips, chair, chocolate)	*Use your fingers to make a beak and go cheep, cheep, cheep.*
th	Thin Theo hurt his thumb on a thistle.	Thin Theo (moth, bath, teeth, tooth, cloth, thimble, third, thank you, thorn)	*Put your thumb to your lips and bite your tongue.*
ng	Bells ring for King Bing ding-dong, ding-dong!	King Bing (ring, wing, song, sling, string, ping-pong, gong)	*Hands on head to make a king's crown.*

7 Blending for reading

The children should practise blending words with Phase Two and new Phase Three graphemes as they work through Phase Three Book 1.

• •

You will need: *sound button words* (▭); *word cards* (▭); *Tog posting box* (▭).

• •

Introductory activities

● Display or write a word on the board, for example, *chin*. Sound talk the word, saying the sounds as you touch or draw in the sound buttons (***ch-i-n***). Say the word. Point to the long sound button under the two-letter grapheme and remind the children that the two letters make one sound. Ask the children to sound and say the word, as you press the sound buttons.

● Display another word. Ask the children to sound talk and say the word together. Make sure that the children say the sounds clearly, recognising any two-letter graphemes and blending the word correctly.

● Display another word. Ask the children to sound and read it with a partner, and raise their hands when they have finished. Sound talk and read the word together.

● Repeat with another word, this time without sound buttons. See whether the children still recognise the two-letter grapheme, say the sounds and blend the word correctly. If not, draw the sound buttons. Ask the children to repeat the sounds after you, as you press the sound buttons.

Sound Phonics activities (pages 5, 15, 21, 27–28, 33)

- In pairs, the children sound, blend and read the words on the page.

- They then match words to pictures (pages 5, 21), identify real and made-up words (pages 15, 33) or find words with a particular grapheme (pages 27, 28).

- On completing the exercises, the children should read the words with a partner, and then with an adult to check their answers.

Note: through repeated reading, the children should begin to read the words automatically without needing to blend. Develop their understanding of word meanings, perhaps asking them to say each word in a sentence.

Extension activities

- Use *sound button words* in group or pair games such as *Pairs* or *In the pot* (see page 15 of this Guide). Children who are more confident with blending could also try *Against the clock* (page 15).

- If the children need more practice at recognising the new grapheme, combine the cards with words containing known graphemes only. Use them in a *Feed Tog* activity (page 15), posting cards with the new grapheme into the *Tog posting box*.

- Use activities where the children have to read and use words. They could read and then draw or mime words, or take part in a treasure hunt where they have to read words and find the corresponding objects.

- Provide opportunities to blend and read words in other areas of learning, perhaps with counting activities (*six chips, six shells*) or shopping lists (*jam, fish, eggs*).

8   Segmenting for spelling

· ·

You will need: *three-box phoneme frame (▢▢); phoneme frame letters (▢▢).*

· ·

Introductory activities

Note: you may use plastic letters for this activity but it is important that individual letters are stuck together to form **sh**, **ch**, **th** *and* **ng***.*

- Display the *three-box phoneme frame* and the set of letters. Say a suitable **CVC word**, for example, *jet* or *chin*. Ask the children to help you say the word in sound talk, with the chopping action if required (**j-e-t, ch-i-n**). Demonstrate finding the letters for each sound and fitting them into the phoneme frame. Sound talk the letters in the frame and say the word.

- Say another word and ask the children to sound talk it with a partner. Involve the children in finding the letter or grapheme to put in the first square of the phoneme frame, then in the second and the third. Repeat with two further words.

- Give the children their own copy of the phoneme frame and the set of letters or graphemes. Say each word in turn. Ask the children to sound the word with a partner and find the letters to build it on the phoneme frame. Check the words together, with everyone sound talking and saying the word.

Sound Phonics activities (pages 6, 16, 29, 34, 37)

- The children sound talk the words to go with the pictures and select the letters required to complete the phoneme frames.

- If the children have difficulty with this activity, encourage them to first sound and build the words on the phoneme frame using *phoneme frame letters* or plastic letters.

Note: *children who are able to write and form letters correctly can write the letters directly on the* **phoneme frame**, *referring to the* **phoneme frame letters**.

Extension activities

- Give the children their own phoneme frame and the set of letters or graphemes needed to make the words on the page. Tell them to swap a letter to make a different word, for example, change *web* to *wet*.

- Continue changing one letter at a time to make a string of words, for example, *vet, jet, bet, bit, wit*. Encourage the children to see how many words they can make. The table below shows the words that can be made with the *phoneme frame letters*.

Sets 1–6	sh and ch	th and ng
bet, bit, jet, job, jot, vet, web, wet, wit	chill, chin, chip, dell, den, dill, din, dip, dish, nip, pen, pill, pin, shed, shell, shin, ship	pang, pat, path, ping, pit, sang, sing, sip, sit, tang, tap, thing, ting, tip, wing, wit, with

Games to practise segmenting for spelling

Spell to win: using *word cards* (⬚) or *sound button words* (⬚), the children choose a word for their partner to spell. If the child spells the word correctly, he or she wins the word card. If not, the partner keeps it.

Applying phonics to spelling

The children should learn to apply their segmenting skills to spell words and to write simple sentences in independent writing activities.

Make sure you demonstrate segmenting to spell words in a range of contexts every day. In shared writing you could write labels, captions, sentences or poems, leaving a word for the children to spell. For example, *Ding dong dell. Can you help me spell 'dell'?*

When writing, encourage the children to orally segment CVC words before writing them down. If they have difficulty remembering the letter needed for a sound, make sure they refer to a copy of the *sound mat* (⬚).

Provide a variety of writing activities so that the children can practise segmenting to spell words. This could include writing or replying to notes from a character in a story or making lists, such as shopping lists, price lists or a register in role play.

Supply a range of writing materials and resources, such as pens and clipboards that can be used inside and outside, or magnetic letters and boards that can be used to make signs.

Encourage the children to think of themselves as writers. Make simple books with blank pages and put these in the writing area so that the children can make their own personal books. Display words that they might wish to use, for example, action words such as *jog* and *sing*, or names of items.

9   Reading sentences

High-frequency words are the words most frequently met when reading. Many of them are **decodable** but some are **tricky words**, which need to be learnt. The children should eventually be able to read all high-frequency words automatically, without needing to sound talk.

You will need: *reading sentence, caption, or question with the focus word* (📖); *words to swap* (📖).

Introductory activities

● Display or write the sentence on the board. Read it together, pointing to each word. Sound talk any unfamiliar but decodable words, such as, *He can f-i-x fix – He can fix the v-a-n van – He can fix the van*. If the sentence is a question or a clue, ask the children to discuss the answer with a partner.

● Read the sentence again and point to the tricky word (*he*). Sound talk the word, putting sound buttons under the phonemes and blending to read the word. Discuss the tricky bit, where the letters do not represent the expected sound (the **e** in *he*) and read the word several times. Point out similarities to other tricky words, for example, *he* and *she*, *no* and *go*.

● Point to the tricky word in the sentence and ask the children to read it, then read the whole sentence with them.

● Change a word in the sentence, keeping the tricky word, or swapping it for a linked tricky word. For example, *He can fix the shed* or *She can fix the van*. Ask the children to read the new sentence with a partner and to raise their hands when they have finished. Read the sentence with the children.

Sound Phonics activities (pages 9–10, 17, 23, 30, 36, 38, 40)

● The children read captions, sentences and questions, selecting the correct answer. Once they have completed the exercises, the children should read the sentences with a partner to check their answers.

● If necessary, support the children by helping them to locate the tricky words in the sentences before they start to read.

Extension activities

● Give a caption or sentence to the children. Cut the text into separate words and ask the children to rebuild it and then read it to a partner.

● Give each pair the set of *words to swap* (📖). Ask them to swap a word in the sentence, and then read the new sentence together to see if it makes sense. The children should see how many sentences they can make.

● The children could then choose a caption or sentence to stick down and illustrate.

● More confident pairs can take it in turns to make a sentence and read it to a partner, who should build it using his or her set of words.

● Refer to the tricky words and high-frequency words throughout the day so that the children learn to recognise them automatically. Look for tricky or high-frequency words in shared or guided reading, perhaps counting how many times they appear on a page.

Applying phonics to reading

Children need plenty of opportunities to apply their phonic skills in a range of contexts. Display signs, captions, labels and notices for the children to read in the learning environment. Ask them to go on 'reading walks' (see page 16 of this Guide) to read ten signs around the classroom.

Other areas of learning can also provide opportunities for the children to apply their phonic knowledge, for example, when reading activity instructions or labels such as *thin things* and *thick things*.

Reading decodable texts

Ensure that reading material is compatible with the children's word-reading skills. **Sound Phonics Rhymes for Reading** provides a selection of decodable rhymes suitable for children working on Phase Three Book 1, as well as **Teaching notes** to help you use the rhymes effectively in the learning environment.

Read an enlarged copy of a rhyme with the group. Demonstrate reading words in context and ask the children to help you with this in some parts of the rhyme. You could also provide individual copies of a rhyme for guided or one-to-one reading. Focus on one or two words from the text at the start of the session, and support the children as they read all or some of the rhyme independently. Make sure that the children have the opportunity to read the rhyme several times so that they read it fluently and can recognise the words. Copies of the rhyme can also be put in reading baskets for independent or paired reading.

You could also create short decodable texts for the children to read. Use the template to make simple *caption books* (📖), with text such as *I can jog, I can fish, I can sing, I can chop* or *A van is big, A jet is big, A bed is big, But a bug is not*. The children can then read and illustrate these books.

A range of reading experiences

Children need opportunities to listen to stories, poems and books that they cannot yet read. This helps them to learn how books and stories work, and how language and fluent reading sound. It will also introduce them to new vocabulary.

Shared reading will often focus on book knowledge or comprehension. However, you could identify a few CVC words featuring recently learnt letters or graphemes and ask the children to read them.

10   Reading words with two parts

Introductory activities

● Write a two-syllable word on the board, for example, *zigzag*. Put a slash between the two **syllables** and add sound buttons. Sound and blend the first syllable and then the second syllable, pressing the sound buttons. Say the word. Sound and blend the word again, asking the children to join in as you press the sound buttons. Repeat with another word, such as *cobweb*.

● Read the poem 'Add zig to a zag' in **Sound Phonics Rhymes for Reading**.

Sound Phonics activities (page 39)

● The children sound, blend and read two-syllable words and match the words to pictures. When they have completed the exercise, the children should read the words with a partner.

Extension activities

● Give the children some two-syllable words to read and illustrate, for example, *rabbit*, *wigwam*.

Sound Phonics Phase Three Book 2

1 Revision

2 Phase Three vowel sounds

3 Blending for reading

4 Segmenting for spelling

5 Reading sentences

6 Reading words with two parts

In Phase Three Book 2, the children consolidate their recognition, recall and formation of the 26 letters, before encountering some two- (and some three-) letter **graphemes** which represent long vowel sounds. Select from the following ideas for 'little and often' practice to use at the start of each session and add new graphemes as they are introduced.

'Little and often' practice

You will need: *grapheme cards* (▭); alphabet frieze; *Phase Two and Three sound mat* (▭); small whiteboards or paper.

Letter or grapheme recognition:

● Hold up the grapheme cards one at a time and ask the children to say the corresponding sound.

● Point to the letters or graphemes on the alphabet frieze or *sound mat* and ask the children to say the sound.

● Write the letters on the board and ask the children to say the sound as soon as the letter is complete.

Letter or grapheme recall:

● Say the sound of a grapheme and ask the children to point to the correct letter on the board or on their *sound mat*.

● Say a letter sound and ask the children to write the letter on a small whiteboard or on paper.

1   Revision: letters and graphemes

. . . .

You will need: *grapheme cards* (▭); *Phase Two and Three sound mat* (▭); the *Stepping stones* game (▭); the *Star blazer* game (▭); counters.

. . . .

Introductory activities

● Use the 'little and often' practice activities described above.

● Display a grapheme card or write the letter on the board. Trace the letter shape with your finger as you say the letter formation patter.

● Ask the children to trace ('finger write') the letter on the carpet or table in front of them and then on a whiteboard.

Sound Phonics activities (page 4)

● Point to the graphemes at random and ask the children to say the sound. Use the grapheme cards and *sound mat* to recap sounds where necessary. Make a note of any letters that still require practice.

● Say a letter sound and ask the children to write over the appropriate letter. The children can do this in pairs, with one child taking the role of teacher.

Extension activities

● Provide a range of writing materials for further letter formation practice. The children may also benefit from using the *Letters* and *Lines* handwriting downloads (⬇).

● Use the *Stepping stones* game to practise letter recognition, or use the *Star blazer* game to practise recognition of Phase Three graphemes towards the end of Phase Three Book 2.

2   Phase Three vowel sounds

In Phase Three Book 2, the children are introduced to two- (and some three-) letter graphemes that represent long vowel sounds.

· ·

You will need: *grapheme card* (▭); *voting paddles* (▭) *with the grapheme on.*

· ·

Introductory activities

● Say the sound, for example, **ai**. Move your hands apart to show the long sound visually. Ask the children to say it with you. Say some words with the sound in them, stretching out the long vowel sound, for example, *pain*, *hail*, *wait*. Ask the children to repeat each word, stretching out the sound and moving their hands.

● Say some words with the long vowel sound and some with a short vowel sound, for example, *rain*, *sail*, *mad*, *maid*. Ask the children to give the thumbs up if they hear the new vowel sound and thumbs down if not.

● Show the grapheme card. Point to the picture and say the word, exaggerating the vowel sound. Point to the grapheme and say the sound, running your finger along the long **sound button**. Explain that the long sound button shows that two (or three) letters stand for one sound.

● Hold up the *voting paddle* a number of times and ask the children to say the sound each time they see it. If it is a sound that can be sustained, such as **oo**, **ee**, **ar**, move the paddle higher or lower and ask the children to vary the volume (or pitch) of the sound accordingly.

● Give out the *voting paddles*. Ask the children to trace over the grapheme with their finger and to say the sound a number of times.

● Write words on the board, some with the new grapheme and some without. Ask the children to hold up the **ai** paddle each time they see a word with the grapheme. Invite the children to underline the new grapheme in the words written on the board.

Sound Phonics activities (pages 5, 7, 10, 12, 15–16, 20, 22, 25, 28, 30, 34, 36, 39)

● In pairs, the children practise saying the sound and then identify items featuring that sound.

● If any children struggle, say the names of the items clearly, exaggerating long vowel sounds. Ask the children to repeat the words after you.

● Children who have learnt the formation of letters can write the grapheme next to the items.

Extension activities

● Use the 'Tell me' game (below) with children who have difficulty identifying or saying the new vowel sounds in words.

> ### Games to practise new vowel sounds
>
> *Tell me:* explain that Tog cannot say words with the new vowel sound. Show an object, such as a bar of soap. Say that Tog pronounces the word *sop*. Ask the children to say the word correctly, emphasising the long vowel sound. Hold up the grapheme card as the children say the sound.

● Reinforce the Phase Three graphemes in other areas of learning, using activities that link the grapheme and its sound. This could include making s**ai**ls for boats and writing **ai** on them, or writing **oo** on ball**oo**ns, **oi** in the s**oi**l and **oa** in s**oa**p or f**oa**m.

● Invent characters to help the children remember some of the graphemes:

   Bart the shark lives f**ar** f**ar** away

   Kurt the t**ur**tle lives in the s**ur**f

   Boo the kangar**oo** who lives in the z**oo**

   Daisy the sn**ai**l who leaves a tr**ai**l

   Tow**ie** the cl**ow**n who is upside d**ow**n.

Use toys or pictures for the characters, giving them badges and *voting paddles* with the grapheme on.

● You could also use examples from familiar stories or everyday contexts, such as Goosey Loosey, *Oodles of Noodles*, *The Baboon who went to the Moon*, The Hoobs™ or Dora the Explorer™.

● Encourage the children to be 'grapheme detectives', looking around the classroom or through a familiar book to identify and write down words containing the sound and grapheme. The children could write the words on shapes that reinforce the sound, for example, **ee** words onto f**ee**t or sw**ee**ts, and **ai** words onto r**ai**ndrops.

---

*Note: the grapheme **ure** is introduced in Phase Three of Letters and Sounds, but is not specifically practised in **Sound Phonics** because there are so few words with this sound. There is a grapheme card for **ure** in the **Teacher's Resource Book** and if you wish, you can introduce this grapheme through words such as p**ure**, c**ure** and s**ure**. For completeness, **ure** is included in the Sound check assessment at the end of Phase Three Book 2, but it should only be assessed if it has been introduced.*

---

3 Blending for reading

The children should practise **blending** to read words with new graphemes as they are introduced. Children often need a lot of practice before they remember to say the long vowel sound rather than the separate letter sounds of a two-letter grapheme (for example, **ai** rather than **a-i**).

You will need: *sound button words with the new grapheme (▢); Tog posting box (▢); voting paddles (▢).*

Introductory activities

● Display a *sound button word*, for example, *nail*. Point out the long sound button under the two-letter grapheme and say the sound. Press each sound button and say the sounds, then the word, for example, *n-ai-l nail*. Ask the children to repeat after you.

● Display another *sound button word* for the children to **sound talk** with you. Pause after saying the sounds and see if the children blend the word.

● Repeat with a few more words, including some with no sound buttons. If the children seem confident, ask them to sound talk and read the words with a partner. Otherwise, continue to sound talk and read together.

● Include one or two words without the new grapheme to make sure that the children are paying close attention to the letters.

Sound Phonics activities (pages 6, 8, 11, 13, 17, 21, 23, 26, 29, 31, 35, 37, 40)

● The children sound, blend and read words, identifying those with the new grapheme. They should read and check the words with a partner and then an adult. Repeated rereading of words will help the children to start reading words automatically.

● For an additional challenge, ask the children to say each of the words featuring the new grapheme in a sentence, to demonstrate that they understand the meanings.

● If necessary, support the children by helping them to touch the sound buttons as they say the sounds. They should run a finger along the long sound button to reinforce the idea that multiple letters can make one sound.

Extension activities

● Use the *sound button words* in pair or small group games, such as *Against the clock*, *In the pot*, *Count on it* or *Pairs* (see page 15 of this Guide), to provide more practice at blending for reading. Children who are confident at recognising graphemes and blending sounds should use word cards without sound buttons.

● For those who need more practice at recognising the graphemes, combine *sound button words* that feature the new grapheme with some that use previously learnt letters. Ask the children to read and sort the words, posting those with the new grapheme into the *Tog posting box*.

● Write lists of words for the children to sound talk and read. Make this into a challenge, for example, read and say each word in a sentence; read and draw the words; read and mime the words.

● Use the word lists in an activity, such as a scavenger hunt or writing a shopping list, or play a game of 'Simon says …' with the last word of each instruction on a *voting paddle*. Look for opportunities to reinforce blending to read words in other areas of learning.

4 Segmenting for spelling

. . . .

You will need: *three- (or two-) box phoneme frame (▭); phoneme frame letters (▭).*

. . . .

Note: *if using plastic letters, stick these together to make two- or three-letter graphemes.*

Introductory activities

● Display the *three-box phoneme frame* and the set of letters. Say a suitable **CVC word** and ask the children to say the word in sound talk.

● Demonstrate finding the graphemes needed for each sound and fitting them into each box on the phoneme frame in turn. Sound talk the letters in the frame and say the word.

● Say another word and ask the children to sound talk it with a partner. Involve the children in finding the letters to put in the phoneme frame.

● Give each child his or her own copy of the phoneme frame and letters. Say each word in turn. Ask the children to sound talk the word and make it on the phoneme frame, using the letters.

Note: *if the children are familiar with forming the letters correctly, they can write directly onto the **phoneme frame**. Model the process, referring to the **phoneme frame letters** as you write each grapheme.*

Sound Phonics activities (pages 9, 18, 27)

● The children should sound talk the words and write the correct graphemes in the phoneme frames. They may use the letters at the top of the page as a model and should sound talk and check their answers with a partner.

● The children could also write the word next to the phoneme frame for extra practice.

● Some children will still need to physically make the words on the phoneme frame before writing them.

Extension activities

● Give each child a copy of the phoneme frame and the set of letters. Ask them to make the words on the page and then swap letters to create more words.

● Children who are able to form the letters correctly can write a list of their words. The table below shows the words that can be made with the *phoneme frame letters*.

ai and ee	oa and oo	ar, or and ur
deep, keel, keep, laid, leek, leer, paid, pail, peek, peel, peer, raid, rail, reed, reek, reel, sail, seed, seek, seep	boat, boot, foal, food, fool, foot, load, loaf, loot, road, roof, root, toad, tool	ark, art, car, carp, cart, cork, far, for, fork, fort, fur, park, part, pork, port, tar

Applying phonics to spelling

Demonstrate segmenting to spell words in a range of contexts. This could include writing sentences and poems in shared writing, or labels and captions in other areas of learning. You could sometimes leave a word for the children to spell, for example, *A horse and cart – can you help me spell 'cart'?*

The children should be able to practise segmenting in real writing situations. Encourage them to make a good attempt at writing the words they want to use. Remind them to orally segment CVC words before writing them down. Allow the children to refer to sound mats (▭) to check the letter or letters that represent a sound, particularly the new long vowel graphemes. Not all spellings will be accurate at this stage but the children should be able to make a good attempt.

Supply a variety of stimulating writing activities to encourage the children to apply their knowledge to segment and spell words. They could write 'get well soon' messages to friends, or birthday greetings to family members.

Provide opportunities to segment and spell words in all areas of learning, for example, writing menus, shopping lists or captions for pictures.

5 Reading sentences

A further six **tricky words** are introduced in Phase Three Book 2. They are introduced and practised through reading sentences, clues and questions.

. . . .

You will need: *reading question, clue or sentence with the tricky word* (▭); *words to swap* (▭); *Tricky word mat one* (▭); *the Beanstalk game* (▭); *counters.*

. . . .

Introductory activities

● Display or write the caption, sentence or question on the board.

● Read the sentence together, pointing to each word. Sound talk one or two phonically **decodable** words that the children do not yet know. For example, *Can you see h-ai-l hail? Can you see hail?* If the sentence is a question or clue, ask the children to discuss their answer with a partner.

● Point to the tricky word in the sentence and read it again, for example, *you.* Write the tricky word on the board. Add sound buttons, and then sound and blend the word, for example, *y-ou you.* Discuss the tricky bit, where the sound does not follow the expected pattern. Point to the word and ask the children to read it a few times, both in and out of the sentence.

● Ask the children to read the whole sentence again, then change one word in the sentence (not the tricky word). The children should read the sentence with a partner and, if it is a question, decide on their answer. Read the new sentence together and discuss the answer if appropriate.

Sound Phonics activities (pages 14, 24, 32, 38, 41–42)

● The children read captions, sentences, clues or questions and select the correct answer. They should then reread the sentences with a partner and check their answers.

- Support the children as necessary, perhaps prompting them to find the tricky word in each sentence before they start to read. Remind the children to look for long vowel graphemes and to read one sentence at a time.

Extension activities

- Give the children a copy of the sentence. Cut it up into separate words and ask the children to rebuild it and read it to their partner. Give each pair the set of *words to swap*. Ask the children to swap a word in the sentence and then read it with a partner to check whether it makes sense. See how many sentences the children can make, then ask them to choose a sentence to stick down and illustrate.

- Refer to the tricky word throughout the day and in shared reading so that the children learn to recognise it. Give the children a copy of the tricky word sentence to read at home.

- **High-frequency** tricky words need lots of practice before children are able to read them automatically. Use *Tricky word mat one*, the *Beanstalk* game and the *Tricky word bookmarks* (▭) to practise and reinforce tricky words introduced so far.

Applying phonics to reading

Children need opportunities to apply their phonic knowledge and skills to read simple texts in a range of meaningful contexts throughout the day. Ensure that any reading materials are compatible with each child's word-reading skills.

Reading in the classroom

Create a rich reading environment with plenty of decodable material, such as posters and labels in role play areas, as well as captions on displays.

Provide a range of simple texts for the children to read in other areas of learning, including facts and simple instructions (for example, *Put the seed in the soil*).

Reading decodable texts

In **Rhymes for Reading** you will find decodable rhymes that the children can read using sounding, blending and their knowledge of tricky words.

Suggestions on how to use these rhymes in group and individual activities are provided on pages 16 and 29 of this Guide, and in the **Teaching notes** in **Rhymes for Reading**. Encourage the children to blend and read words featuring recently introduced graphemes. Help them to do this if they get stuck on a word as they read the rhyme.

Provide opportunities to reread the rhyme a number of times. Put copies of the rhyme in reading baskets for independent reading, or ask the children to read it to a partner.

Although the focus is on decoding, always ask some simple questions to check whether the children understand what they have read. It is important for the children to recognise that reading is not just about decoding words but also about understanding what those words mean in context.

Use the *caption book* template (▭) to make simple decodable books that the children can read and illustrate. These could be particular to the children, for example, *Tanya on the farm*; *Tanya at the zoo*, or linked to current areas of interest, such as *a shark has sharp teeth*; *a cow has a long tail*.

Shared reading

Children need opportunities to listen to stories, poems and other books that they cannot yet read for themselves. For more information, see pages 16 and 29 of this Guide.

At this stage you could also identify an occasional word, phrase or sentence you want the children to blend and read. Mark these, so that the children know to sound and blend these words as they reach them.

6   Reading words with two parts

. . . .

You will need: *word cards* (📖).

. . . .

Introductory activities

● Say some two-syllable words, clapping each **syllable**. Ask the children to join in.

● Display a two-syllable word on the board, for example, *raincoat*. Put a slash between the two syllables, for example, *rain/coat*. Sound and blend the first syllable (*r-ai-n rain*) and then the second syllable (*c-oa-t coat*). Say the word (*raincoat*). Repeat the process with the children.

● Write another word on the board and repeat the process.

Sound Phonics activities (pages 19, 33)

● The children sound, blend and read two-syllable words and then match the words to the pictures. When they have finished, the children should read the words with a partner to check their answers.

● If any of the children need support, talk them through the process as described above.

Extension activities

● Give the children the word cards to practise reading two-part words. Ask them to read each word with a partner, and then say it in a sentence or draw a picture to show the meaning of the word.

● If the children need support with two-part words, put in a slash between the syllables.

Sound Phonics Phase Four

1 Revising graphemes

2 Reading familiar high-frequency words

3 Introducing CVCC and CCVC words

4 Blending CVCC and CCVC words

5 Segmenting for spelling: CVCC and CCVC words

6 Reading sentences with tricky words

7 Spelling tricky words

8 Reading words with two parts

There are no new **graphemes** in Phase Four, but it is important to consolidate knowledge of the graphemes introduced so far and to ensure that all letters are formed correctly. Make 'little and often' practice a regular part of phonics sessions, using the activities described on page 31 of this Guide.

1   Revising graphemes

You will need: *Phase Two and Phase Three sound mat* (▭); *Phase Three sound mat* (▭); *grapheme cards* (▭); the *Stepping stones* game (▭); the *Star blazer* game (▭); *counters*.

Introductory activities

● Use the 'little and often' practice activities, as described on page 31 of this Guide.

● Say a sound and ask the children to write the corresponding letter. Say the formation patter as they write the letter.

Sound Phonics activities (pages 4, 5, 27)

● On page 4, say a letter sound and ask the children to find and write over the letter. They can use different colours to write over the letters several times, creating 'rainbow letters'.

● On pages 5 and 27, point to the graphemes at random and ask the children to say the corresponding sound.

● The children can practise these activities in pairs, with one child taking the role of the adult.

● Those who have difficulty with letter formation can use a range of writing materials for additional practice, referring to page 4 or the *Letters* handwriting download (▭) if necessary.

Extension activities

● Use the *Phase Two* and *Phase Three sound mats* to support the children's recognition and recall of letters and graphemes when reading and writing.

● Use grapheme cards or the *Stepping stones* game to practise letter recognition. The *Star blazer* game or grapheme cards may be used to practise recognition of Phase Three graphemes.

2   Reading familiar high-frequency words

Both **decodable** and **tricky high-frequency words** need to be practised so that the children can read them automatically as early as possible. They should regularly practise reading groups of decodable high-frequency words (and familiar tricky words) as they proceed through Phase Four, so that they are able to recognise them instantly.

You will need: *blank word cards* (▭); *Against the clock cards* (▭).

Introductory activities

● Use *blank word cards* to make high-frequency word cards, or use the *Against the clock* cards. Hold up a word card and see if the children read it automatically. If not, **sound talk** the word and read it together. Repeat this for all the words.

● Display the words again in a different order, encouraging the children to read them automatically if possible. Repeat, increasing the pace for a rapid response.

Sound Phonics activities (page 8)

● Time the children to see how long they need to read the words on the page, or see how many words they can read before a timer runs out. Times can be recorded on the page so that the children can try to beat their score at a later date.

Extension activities

● The children could play *Against the clock* (see page 15 of this Guide) in pairs, adding the Phase Four cards to those used in Phase Three. The Phase Four *Against the clock* cards are located at the end of the Phase Four resources in the **Teacher's Resource Book**. The children should turn over the cards and see how many they can read before the timer runs out.

3   Introducing CVCC and CCVC words

The main focus of Phase Four is **blending** and **segmenting** words with **adjacent consonants**.

∙∙

You will need: *grapheme cards (▭) or plastic letters.*

∙∙

Introductory activities

Introducing CVCC words:

● On the board, write the word *den*. Ask the children to sound and blend the word (*d-e-n* den).

● Add **t** to the end of the word and sound talk the word again. Hold the **n** sound so that it blends into **t** (*d-e-nnn-t* dent). Repeat with the children.

● Repeat the same process with other words, for example, *ten/**t**, ban/**d**.*

Introducing CCVC words:

● On the board, write the word *nap*. Ask the children to sound and blend the word (*n-a-p* nap).

● Add **s** to the start of the word and sound talk the word again. Hold the **s** sound so it blends into **n** (*sss-n-a-p* snap). Repeat with the children.

● Repeat the same process with other words, for example, *s/top, t/rip.*

Sound Phonics activities (pages 6, 9, 16, 28)

● The children sound talk and read **CVC words**. They extend each word by adding an extra consonant and then read the new **CVCC** or **CCVC words**.

● Once they have read the words, the children should join with a partner and read the words again, saying each word in a sentence.

Extension activities

● Use grapheme cards or plastic letters to build more words with adjacent consonants, such as *drip* or *flap*.

4 Blending CVCC and CCVC words

. . . .

You will need: *sound button words* with adjacent consonants (⬚).

. . . .

Introductory activities

● Display a *sound button word*, or write the word on the board and draw in the **sound buttons**. Say the sounds as you press each sound button and blend to make the word. Ask the children to repeat the process.

● Display another word. Ask the children to sound talk it together and then say the word.

● Display another word and ask the children to sound talk it with a partner and raise their hands when they have read it. Make sure that the children are blending the words successfully.

Sound Phonics activities (pages 10–11, 17–18, 22, 29–30, 35)

● The children sound, blend and read the words. They select the correct word to match a picture or identify real words and made-up words.

● The children should then work with a partner to sound talk and read the words, and then check their answers.

● Some children may find it difficult to blend four or five sounds, particularly if they say the sounds slowly. Support these children by repeating the sounds more quickly to see if it helps them to orally blend the word.

Extension activities

● Use the *sound button words* to provide more practice at blending words with consonant clusters. The children could play *Pairs*, *In the pot* or *Count on it* (see page 15 of this Guide).

● Confident children could see how many of the words they can sound, blend and read before the timer runs out. This is a good activity for building up speed and confidence at blending to read words.

● Add labels around the classroom and role play area featuring words with consonant clusters, such as *stamps*, *cards* and *rubber bands* in the post office.

5 Segmenting for spelling: CVCC and CCVC words

. . . .

You will need: *enlarged four-box phoneme frame* (⬚); *enlarged phoneme frame letters* (⬚); *small four-box phoneme frame* (⬚); *small phoneme frame letters* (⬚); *sound button words* (⬚).

. . . .

Introductory activities

● Say a suitable CVCC or CCVC word, for example, *hand* or *pram*, and then say it in sound talk. Exaggerate the penultimate consonant in CVCC words or second consonant in CCVC words (*h-a-**n**-d*, *p-**r**-a-m*).

● Say it again, counting the sounds by raising a finger for each of the four sounds. Ask the children to repeat after you.

● Say some other words for the children to say in sound talk, reminding them to count the sounds on their fingers. Make sure that the children are clearly separating the two letters in the consonant cluster and counting four sounds. If not, model the process again and ask the children to repeat after you.

● Display the enlarged *four-box phoneme frame* and letters. Demonstrate making three of the words on the phoneme frame. Involve the children in finding the letters to put in each space.

● Give the children their own copies of the phoneme frame and the set of letters. Ask them to make the same words. Say another word for the children to sound and make.

Sound Phonics activities (pages 12, 19, 31, 39)

● The children sound talk words and write in the letters needed to complete the phoneme frames. They then check their answers with a partner by sound talking and reading what they have written. Page 7 can also be used for revision of CVC words.

● If the children have difficulty with segmenting the separate sounds in a consonant cluster, help them to count the sounds on their fingers. With CVCC words, it can help to say or segment the first three sounds and then add the last letter, for example, *lamp **l-a-m** (p)*.

Extension activities

● Some of the children may have difficulty hearing and segmenting the two sounds in adjacent consonants, spelling words such as *went* as *wet* or *pond* as *pod*. Try the *Tell me* activity (page 33 of this Guide) with these children. Focus on consonant sounds, mispronouncing *frog* as *fog*, for example.

● For further practice, use *sound button words* in pair or group spelling games, such as *Spell to win* (page 27 of this Guide).

● Children who are able to segment and spell the words in the activity book can use a copy of the phoneme frame and letters to make more words. The table below shows the words that can be made with each set of letters. Words indicated in bold will require the *three-box phoneme frame*.

CVCC words	CCVC words	CVCC and CCVC words
and, **ant**, **ask**, band, bend, bent, best, dent, desk, **end**, hand, land, last, lend, lent, nest, sand, send, sent, task, tend	flag, flan, flap, flat, flip, flit, gran, grim, grin, grip, grit, plan, pram, prim, tram, trap, trim, trip	belt, bend, bent, best, bled, braid, brain, brown, dent, drain, drown, lend, nest, rest, send, sent, snail, stain, tend, trail, train

6   Reading sentences with tricky words

In Phase Four a further fourteen tricky words are introduced. These are encountered in the context of reading clues, sentences and questions.

• •

You will need: *reading sentence or question with the tricky word* (▢▢)*; words to swap* (▢▢)*; Tricky word mat two* (▢▢)*; the Chimney game* (▢▢)*; counters.*

• •

Introductory activities

● Display or write the caption, sentence or question on the board.

● Read the sentence, pointing to each word. Sound talk one or two less familiar words, for example, *I l-o-s-t lost* – *"I lost my sh-ee-p sheep,"* – *"I lost my sheep," she said*. If the sentence is a question or a clue, ask the children to discuss the answer with a partner.

● Point to the new tricky word in the sentence, for example, *said*, and read it again. Write the word on the board. Sound talk it, putting sound buttons under the **phonemes** (*s-ai-d said*). Discuss the tricky bit, where the sound does not follow the expected pattern. Point to the word both in and out of the sentence and ask the children to read it.

● Read the complete sentence again, then change one word in the sentence, for example, *"I lost my slipper," she said*. Ask the children to read the new sentence with a partner. When everyone has done this, read it together.

● Point out any patterns in tricky words, such as, *so, no, go* or *some* and *come*.

Sound Phonics activities (pages 13, 15, 20–21, 23–24, 32–33, 36–37, 40, 42)

● The children read captions, sentences, clues and questions, selecting the correct answer or drawing pictures to fit the text. They should then read the sentences with a partner and check their answers.

● Support the children as necessary, perhaps reading one sentence at a time, finding the tricky word before reading, or helping them to blend words with adjacent consonants.

Extension activities

● Cut a copy of the sentence into separate words. Ask the children to rebuild it and read it to a partner to see if it makes sense.

● In pairs, the children should change one word to make a new sentence to read. They could see how many different sentences they can make, or choose a sentence to stick down and illustrate.

● Children who are confident at writing can read the sentence a few times, 'hold it in their head' and then try writing it. They can then compare their version with the original.

● Refer to the tricky word throughout the day and in shared reading so that the children learn to recognise it. Give them a copy of the tricky word sentence to read at home.

● High-frequency tricky words need plenty of practice so that the children are able to read them automatically. Use *Tricky word mat two* and the *Chimney* game to consolidate tricky words introduced in Phase Four.

● *Tricky word bookmarks* (▭) can be slipped into reading books for regular practice at school and home.

Applying phonics to reading

Children need to apply their phonic knowledge and skills to reading a range of material in different contexts and settings. As well as guided or one-to-one reading, there should be opportunities to read in free choice activities, role play and other areas of learning. Make sure that reading material is interesting and engaging but also appropriate to the children's level of reading.

Reading in the classroom

Create phonically decodable reading material to incorporate in the classroom environment and classroom activities. This could include:

● Signs to help the children find or put things away in the correct place
I put my lunchbox on the shelf.

● Captions on displays of work and photographs
Look! We can swim.

● Instructions in different subject areas
Next add a spoon of milk.

● Factual texts, such as *caption books* (▭), linked to current topics and themes
We get milk from cows. We get eggs from hens. We get wool from sheep.

● Personalised *caption books* for the children to read and illustrate
Stella has black hair, Stella has a red dress.

● Signs, notices and posters in role play areas
cash desk, fresh milk, Let me help you.

Shared reading

Use shared reading to model fluent reading. Occasionally demonstrate decoding an unfamiliar word by sounding and blending it, or select a word or phrase containing adjacent consonants for the children to read. Mark it so that the children know it is their turn.

Guided reading

Guided reading is a useful opportunity to ensure that the children apply phonic knowledge and skills to reading texts such as short books or complete poems. Select texts that offer opportunities to use recently practised skills, such as reading new tricky words or words with adjacent consonants. The text should have a good proportion of known words but also some 'challenge words' which require the children to apply new learning.

A selection of decodable rhymes suitable for this stage can be found in **Sound Phonics Rhymes for Reading**, along with **Teaching notes** to help you use the rhymes effectively in the learning environment.

When introducing a text in guided reading, remind the children of any graphemes, words or skills that they have been learning. Explain that they will need to use these to understand the text. As the children read, prompt them to apply their knowledge and skills to work out unfamiliar words.

Although guided reading sessions may still have a large element of phonics at this stage, it is important that the children have the chance to respond to the subject matter as well. Ensure that there are always opportunities to respond to the text and to discuss word meanings and ideas in guided reading sessions.

The children should always be able to reread the texts they have read in guided sessions. This can be silently or aloud, by themselves or with a partner or adult. This helps to improve their fluency and increases their familiarity with words. Books and poems can be collected in reading baskets and always made available to pupils for this purpose.

7 Spelling tricky words

High-frequency words are not only found in texts that children read – they are also the words that children are most likely to use when writing. Tricky words with unusual spellings are the most problematic and need to be learnt. The children should be able to read these tricky words before they are expected to spell them.

You will need: *small whiteboards or paper; Tricky word mat one* (📖).

Introductory activities

● Write a short sentence on the board using the tricky word, for example, *I was lost*. Ask the children to read it. Underline the tricky word to be learnt and read it again.

● Sound talk the word, pointing to each grapheme as you say the sound. Discuss the tricky part of the word, for example, the **o** sound in *was*.

● Ask the children to trace ('finger write') the word on the carpet or table in front of them a few times. Rub the word off the board and ask the children to write it on their whiteboards or paper. Check the spellings.

● Ask the children to write a short sentence using the word, such as, *I was fast*.

● Draw their attention to any patterns in tricky words, such as *he*, *she*, *we*, *me*, *be* or *the*, *they*.

Sound Phonics activities (pages 14, 25, 34, 41)

● The children practise spelling the words and using them to complete sentences.

● The children should then turn the book over and see if they can write the tricky word correctly. They should do this three times.

Extension activities

● Confident spellers can write their own sentences using the tricky word.

● Children who have difficulty remembering spellings may benefit from writing the word several times with a range of writing materials.

● As soon as they have learnt how to spell a tricky word, the children should use the correct spelling in their own writing. Support them by giving each child a copy of *Tricky word mat one*. Encourage the children to check their spellings rather than spell the word incorrectly. Gradually they should retain the correct spelling without needing to refer to the mat.

● Provide opportunities to use the tricky words in all areas of learning. This could include writing messages, captions or short texts about things that the children have done.

Applying phonics to writing

By this stage, the children should be able to make a phonically plausible attempt at writing many of the words they want to use. They may still have some difficulty recalling the Phase Three vowel graphemes and should have a copy of the *Phase Three sound mat* (▭) to refer to when writing.

Shared writing

Leave two or three words for the children to spell, perhaps tricky words that they have learnt recently, or words with adjacent consonants. Ask the children to segment the word, counting the sounds on their fingers, and then to say the sounds or tell you which letters to write.

Guided writing

Encourage the children to orally segment words with adjacent consonants before they write them, counting the sounds on their fingers. Praise any attempts where spellings are phonically plausible and in accordance with current knowledge, even if you have to give the children the correct spelling.

Provide activities that encourage writing and spelling words in all areas of learning, for example, writing labels for models or collections that the children have made, writing in response to experiences, or writing captions for pictures.

Always have a variety of writing materials available in the writing area, including empty *caption books* (▭) for the children to fill in. In all independent writing, the children should refer to sound mats (▭) if they cannot remember the grapheme for a sound, and to tricky word mats (▭) to check the spelling of tricky words.

8 Reading words with two parts

You will need: *word cards* (▭).

Introductory activities

● Say some two-part words and clap each **syllable** with the children. Word cards for Phase Four two-part words are located at the end of the Phase Three resources in the **Teacher's Resource Book**.

● As in Phase Three, write a two-part word on the board, for example, *desktop*. Put a slash between the two syllables, for example, *desk/top*.

● Sound and blend the first syllable (*d-e-s-k desk*) and then the second syllable (*t-o-p top*). Say the word (*desktop*). Repeat the process with the children.

● Write another word on the board and repeat this process.

Sound Phonics activities (pages 26, 38)

● The children sound, blend and read two-part words and then match the words to the pictures. They should read the words with a partner to check their answers.

● If the children need support, talk them through the process again.

Extension activities

● Give the word cards for two-part words to the children to practise reading. Ask them to read the words in pairs. They should say each word in a sentence or choose words to stick down and illustrate.

● If the children need support with reading two-part words, draw a slash between the syllables.

Sound Phonics Phase Five Book 1

1 Revising Phase Three graphemes

2 Blending to read words

3 Spelling: counting phonemes

4 Reading familiar high-frequency words

5 Introducing new graphemes

6 Reading sentences with tricky words

7 Spelling words with two parts

8 Writing sentences with tricky words

9 Split digraphs and graphemes

In Phase Five Book 1, the children encounter more new **graphemes**, although they will still need 'little and often' practice of known graphemes (particularly the two- and three-letter graphemes introduced in Phase Three). This will help the children to quickly recognise and recall graphemes with more than one letter when reading, as well as when spelling. Phase Five graphemes can be added to the 'little and often' practice as they are introduced.

1 Revising Phase Three graphemes

You will need: *grapheme cards* (▢); *Phase Three sound mat* (▢); *small whiteboards or paper; the* Star blazer *game* (▢); *the* Treasure trail *game* (▢); *counters.*

Introductory activities

● Following the suggestions on page 31 of this Guide, use grapheme cards and the sound mat to consolidate knowledge of Phase Three graphemes.

Sound Phonics activities (pages 4, 23)

● Point to the graphemes and ask the children to say the sounds. This can also be reversed, saying a sound and asking the children to point to the grapheme. Refer to the grapheme cards or *sound mat* if required.

● The children can practise this in pairs, with one child taking the role of the adult. Those who still need the support of picture prompts can practise in pairs with a set of grapheme cards or a sound mat (as described on page 31 of this Guide).

Extension activities

● To practise recognition of Phase Three graphemes, use the *Star blazer* game. The *Treasure trail* game can also be used towards the end of Phase Five Book 1, once new graphemes have been introduced.

● Sound mats may be sent home to reinforce recognition and recall of graphemes.

2 Blending to read words

Children should now be familiar with the **blending** process, but they may still need practice at recognising two-letter graphemes or blending longer words. Revise this at the start of Phase Five Book 1 using Phase Three graphemes and words with **adjacent consonants**, before introducing the new graphemes.

You will need: *Phase Three and Phase Four word cards without sound buttons* (▢).

Introductory activities

● Display a word. Ask the children to **sound talk** and say the word together. If they do not recognise a two-letter grapheme, draw a long **sound button** under it and sound talk again.

● Repeat with more words, supporting the children if necessary. Check that they say just one sound for two- or three-letter graphemes.

Sound Phonics activities (page 5)

● The children draw sound buttons, then blend and read the words on the page, matching the words to pictures.

Extension activities

● If further practice is needed in blending, select more word cards for Phase Three Book 2 and Phase Four. Use words without sound buttons but let the children add them if necessary.

● The children can practise in pairs or use the word cards in games such as *Count on it*, *Pairs*, or *In the pot* (see page 15 of this Guide). More confident children could try *Against the clock* (page 15). Remind the children that if they recognise a word they do not need to sound and blend it.

3   Spelling: counting phonemes

In Phase Five, it is important that children consolidate their **segmenting** skills so that they can spell words with adjacent consonants and familiar graphemes. There are two elements that they need to practise – segmenting and counting the sounds, and choosing the appropriate grapheme to represent the sounds.

Consolidation of Phase Three graphemes will help the children to make phonically plausible attempts at words. As they learn more graphemes, they will be able to choose the correct spellings for many familiar words.

. . . .

You will need: *two-, three-, four- and five-box phoneme frames (▢▢); phoneme frame letters (▢▢) or plastic letters; Phase Three (or Phase Five) sound mat (▢▢); small whiteboards or paper.*

. . . .

Note: *if using plastic letters, stick these together to make two- or three-letter graphemes.*

Introductory activities

● Display the phoneme frames. Say a word and ask the children to say it in sound talk, counting the **phonemes** on their fingers. Ask the children to point to the phoneme frame needed for that word.

● Demonstrate writing the graphemes on the phoneme frame, using the *sound mat* to find the correct grapheme for the vowel sound. Ask children to say the sounds and write the word on their whiteboards or paper.

● Repeat with words containing different numbers of phonemes, for example, *now*, *crisp*, *teach*. If the children are confident, they can sound and count the phonemes with a partner, then write the words on a whiteboard. If not, continue to discuss and write the words on the phoneme frame together before asking the children to write them down.

Sound Phonics activities (pages 6, 13, 35)

● The children sound and count the phonemes, and write words to go with the pictures. They should then sound talk and check their spellings with a partner.

- Children who need further practice at segmenting will benefit from building the words on phoneme frames before they write them.

- If the children have difficulty remembering the appropriate grapheme, remind them to refer to the *sound mat*.

Extension activities

- Word cards that have previously been used for reading activities can now be used for additional practice at spelling words.

- Give the children the *two-*, *three-*, *four-* and *five-box phoneme frames* and letters. They should see how many words they can make and then write them down. A list of possible words is given below.

Two phonemes	Three phonemes	Four phonemes
each, eat, sea, tea	beach, beam, bean, beat, cheat, east, lean, meal, mean, meat, neat, seal, seam, seat, teach, team	beans, beast, beats, least, meals, steal, steam

Games to practise segmenting for spelling

Guess my word: one child takes a word card (without showing it) and gives a clue to the word. The partner writes the word and the children check the spelling together.

4   Reading familiar high-frequency words

The children will need to practise both **tricky** and **decodable high-frequency words** regularly until they are able to read them automatically.

You will need: *blank word cards* (▭) or *Against the clock* cards (▭); the *Chimney game* (▭); counters.

Introductory activities

- Use *blank word cards* to make high-frequency word cards, or use the *Against the clock* cards. Display a word card. See if the children read it automatically. If not, ask them to sound and read the word. Say the word in a sentence.

- Repeat for all the word cards, then display them in a different order. Encourage the children to say the words automatically without sound talking.

Sound Phonics activities (page 7)

- Time how long the children need to read the words on the page. Alternatively, count the number of words that they can read before a timer runs out. Note the time or score on the page so that the children can try to beat it at a later date. The children can practise this activity in pairs.

Extension activities

- For further practice at reading the Phase Four tricky words, use the *Chimney* game.

- *Tricky word bookmarks* (▭) can be placed in reading books or taken home for regular practice of the tricky words introduced in Phases Three and Four.

5 Introducing new graphemes

By Phase Five children often learn new graphemes quickly, so these can be introduced at a rapid pace through word-reading activities.

. . . .

You will need: *grapheme card* (▭); *word cards with the new grapheme* (▭).

. . . .

Introductory activities

- Show the grapheme card. Point to the picture and say the word, exaggerating the new sound, for example, **tray.** Point to the grapheme and say the sound. Run your finger under the grapheme and say the sound again, then say the word. Ask the children to repeat after you.

- Show a word card featuring the grapheme or write it on the board. Underline the new grapheme and ask the children to sound and read the word.

- Repeat with two or three more words, but do not underline the grapheme. See if the children can identify and say the new grapheme, for example, saying **p-l-ay** *play* not **p-l-a-y**. If the children find this difficult, underline the new grapheme and then sound and blend the word together.

Sound Phonics activities (pages 9–12, 17–20, 24–27, 39–40)

- The children write in the new grapheme and read the words. They then match the words to the pictures, or decide whether the words are real or made up.

- The children should then read the words with a partner and check their answers. They should say any real words aloud in sentences.

- If the children find the activity difficult, help them to draw sound buttons under the letters as they say the sounds. If necessary, repeat the sound talk back to them and see if they can orally blend the word.

Extension activities

- Use word cards to give more practice at recognising graphemes and reading words. The children take it in turns to sound and read a word to a partner, who says it in a sentence to show that he or she understands its meaning.

- Use the words in partner games so that the children become familiar with them. If the children recognise a word, there is no need to sound and blend it, but they should still sound and blend any unfamiliar words.

- Most of the children should now be able to read words without sound buttons. If some children have difficulty recognising the new graphemes or saying the sounds, help them to add sound buttons under new words when they first read them.

Games to practise new graphemes

Grapheme hunt: the children should search for words with the grapheme and write them on appropriate paper shapes, for example, **ou** on cl**ou**ds and **ea** on l**ea**ves. These will be useful when the children start to spell words with these graphemes.

6 Reading sentences with tricky words

Nine more tricky words are introduced in Phase Five Book 1, in the context of reading sentences and questions.

You will need: *reading sentence or question with the tricky word* (📖); *words to swap* (📖).

Introductory activities

- Display or write the sentence or question on the board. Read the sentence with the children, pointing to each word.

- Encourage the children to read an unfamiliar but decodable word, such as, *Oh dear I have lost my **s-c-ar-f** scarf.* Reread the complete sentence together. If it is a question, the children should discuss the answer with a partner.

- Point to the new tricky word (*oh*) and read the sentence again. Write the tricky word on the board and sound talk it (if possible), pointing to the graphemes. Discuss the 'tricky' bit, where letters do not represent the expected sound.

- Ask the children to read the word a few times, both in and out of the sentence.

- Read the complete sentence again, then change one word, for example, *Oh dear I have lost my cloak.* Ask the children to read the sentence with a partner and to raise their hands when they have finished. Read the sentence together, and if it is a question, discuss the answer.

Note: Mr and Mrs cannot be sound talked. Instead write the full word Mister and show that Mr is a shortened way of writing it: rub out the middle letters and push **M** and **r** together.

Sound Phonics activities (pages 8, 14, 21, 28, 36, 41)

- The children read sentences and questions, selecting the correct answer or matching the sentences to pictures. They should then read the sentences with a partner to check their answers.

Extension activities

- Refer to the tricky word throughout the day and in shared and guided reading so that the children learn to recognise it.

- Cut up the sentence and give a copy to each child, along with the *words to swap*. Ask the children to change one word in the sentence and to read the new sentence with their partner. See how many 'sensible' sentences they can make. They could also choose a sentence to stick down and illustrate.

- Confident writers can say the sentence a few times, 'hold it in their head' and then try to write it. They should then compare their version with the original sentence.

- Copies of the tricky word sentence can also be taken home for practice.

Applying phonics to reading

Shared reading

Plan opportunities for the children to use their new phonic knowledge and skills to blend and read a few words or phrases in each text.

Guided reading

Select texts appropriate to the children's knowledge and abilities. Prompt the children to use their phonic skills and their knowledge of graphemes to read the texts.

Provide opportunities across the curriculum and throughout the learning environment to apply phonic knowledge and skills to independent reading and writing activities.

7   Spelling words with two parts

You will need: *word cards* (▭); *small whiteboards or paper.*

Introductory activities

- Recap reading two-part words. Write a word on the board, for example, *playpen*. Ask the children how they would read this word. Sound and blend the first **syllable** (*p-l-ay*) and then the second syllable (*p-e-n*), before saying the word (*playpen*).

- Explain that spelling a two-part word is the reverse process. Say the sounds in the first syllable and write *p-l-ay*. Say the sounds in the second syllable and write *p-e-n*. Read the word.

- Ask the children to say the sounds and to write the word on their whiteboard or paper.

- Say some more two-part words and ask the children to clap and say each syllable. Say the sounds and write the letters for the first and second syllables, as before.

Sound Phonics activities (pages 15, 37)

- The children say the two syllables in compound words as separate words and write in the missing syllable, using the picture clues to help.

Extension activities

- One child should pick up a word card and read it to his or her partner, who then checks it and says the word in a sentence. Both children should sound the syllables, then write the graphemes.

8 Writing sentences with tricky words

Some of the words that children use most frequently when writing are tricky words with unusual spellings. These need to be taught before the children learn an incorrect spelling (for example, *sed* instead of *said*).

***

Note: children must be able to read these tricky words before they are expected to spell them.

***

You will need: *writing sentence or caption with the tricky word (▭); small whiteboards or paper; Tricky word mat three (▭).*

Introductory activities

● Write the tricky word on the board, for example, *some*. Ask the children to read it. Say the word in a sentence, such as, *Put some books on a shelf.* Sound talk the word, pointing to the graphemes (**s-o-me**). Discuss the tricky part, in this case the **me** ending on *some*.

● Ask the children to trace ('finger write') the word a few times on the carpet or table in front of them. Rub the word off the board and ask the children to write it down. Check the spelling and repeat.

● Ask the children to write a short sentence using the word, for example, *Some books go on a shelf.*

● Draw attention to helpful patterns in tricky words, for example, *some* and *come*, *were* and *there*.

Sound Phonics activities (pages 16, 22, 29, 38, 42)

● The children practise spelling the words and using them in complete sentences. They should then close the book and see if they can write the tricky word correctly.

Extension activities

● Give the children a copy of the tricky word sentence. They should read the sentence aloud a few times with a partner and hold it in their heads. The children then turn the sentence over and say it one word at a time as they write it down. They can then check it against the original. Confident spellers could write their own sentences using the tricky word.

● When the children have learnt to spell a tricky word, they should use the correct spelling whenever they write. Provide opportunities for the children to use the new tricky word across all subject areas. For example, you could use *some* to write captions (*We had some seeds*) or lists of materials (*I will need: some card, some string*), or to make simple factual *caption books* (▭) (*Some dogs are big; Some dogs run fast*).

● Display the Phase Five Book 1 tricky words and encourage the children to use the *tricky word mat* to help them to spell the words. Gradually the words can be taken down as the children retain the correct spelling.

Applying phonics to writing

The children should be able to make a good attempt at spelling many words using their knowledge of segmenting. Not all spellings will be accurate at this stage, but they should be phonically plausible. Give sound mats (📖) to the children to refer to when they are writing. You could also display these in the classroom.

Shared writing

Ask the children to help you to segment and spell two or three words to reinforce the process and to revise particular graphemes. Plan writing activities that will use known tricky words and graphemes.

9 Split digraphs and graphemes

The split digraphs (**a-e**, **e-e**, **i-e**, **o-e**, **u-e**) are sometimes introduced as the 'magic e'. In phonics terms they are still digraphs (two letters that make one sound), but on this occasion the letters are not directly next to one another. The idea of a split digraph is best demonstrated physically using other known graphemes, for example, relating **i-e** to **ie**.

You will need: *four white voting paddles (📖) with p, n, l or d on each; one coloured voting paddle (📖) with ie on; word cards (📖).*

Introductory activities

- Ask one child to hold the **p** paddle and another child to hold the **ie** paddle, spelling *pie*. The rest of the children should sound talk the word.

- Ask the children what they would need to add to turn *pie* into *pine*. Sound talk the word and ask another child to hold the **n** paddle at the end, spelling *p-ie-n*.

- Explain that in this word, **ie** is a split grapheme. Cut the **ie** paddle in half, creating **i** and **e** separately. The child holding the **ie** paddle should now hold the two half paddles (**i** and **e**), with one arm around the back of the child holding **n**, spelling *p-i-n-e*.

- Use the coloured half paddles to demonstrate that the **i** and the **e** still make just one sound. Repeat with other words, for example, *lie* (*line*), *pie* (*pile*), *die* (*dine*).

Sound Phonics activities (pages 30–34)

- The children write the split digraph and read the words. They then match the words to the pictures or decide whether the words are real or made up.

- Each child should then read the words with a partner and check their answers. They should say any real words aloud in sentences.

Extension activities

- Use the word cards to provide more practice at recognising graphemes and reading words. In pairs, the children take it in turns to sound talk and read a word. The partner should say the word in a sentence to demonstrate that he or she understands its meaning.

Sound Phonics Phase Five Book 2

1   Revising graphemes

2   Reading familiar high-frequency words

3   Reading words with Phase Five graphemes

4   Spelling: counting phonemes

5   Reading and spelling words with two parts

6   Reading questions with tricky words

7   Alternative pronunciations of graphemes

8   Reading sentences with alternative pronunciations of graphemes

9   Writing sentences with tricky words

10 Homographs

11 Reading a story with tricky words

Children should continue the 'little and often' practice of Phase Three and Five **graphemes** so that these can be used readily in reading and spelling. Alternative pronunciations of some graphemes can be included as they are learnt.

1   Revising graphemes

You will need: *grapheme cards* (▭); *Phase Three* or *Phase Five sound mats* (▭); the *Star blazer* game (▭); the *Treasure trail* game (▭); *counters.*

Introductory activities

● Following the suggestions for 'little and often' practice on page 31 of this Guide, use the grapheme cards and *sound mat* to consolidate the children's understanding of Phase Three and Five graphemes.

● Make this into a fun, fast-paced activity requiring immediate response.

Sound Phonics activities (pages 4, 5, 23, 31)

● Point to the graphemes and ask the children to say the sounds. Alternatively, say a sound and ask the children to point to the grapheme.

● The children can practise in pairs, with one child taking the role of the adult. Use the grapheme cards and *sound mat* to prompt the children if necessary.

Extension activities

● Use the *Star blazer* game for further practice of Phase Three graphemes and *Treasure trail* game for Phase Five graphemes.

2   Reading familiar high-frequency words

In order to develop confidence and fluency when reading texts, it is important that the children can read **high-frequency words** automatically (both **decodable** and **tricky**). Reading a group of these words every day will help the children to recognise them immediately when reading.

You will need: *blank word cards* (▭) or *Against the clock* cards (▭); the *Chimney* game (▭); the *Maze* game (▭); *counters.*

Introductory activities

● Use *blank word cards* to make high-frequency word cards, or use the *Against the clock* cards. Hold up a word card and see if the children read the word automatically. If not, ask them to **sound talk** and read it. Repeat with all the words. Remind the children that this is not always possible with tricky words (see note on page 52 of this Guide).

● Hold up the words in a different order, encouraging the children to say them automatically if possible. Repeat a third time, saying the children's names as you hold up each word.

Sound Phonics activities (page 6)

● Time the children to see how long they need to read the words on the page, or see how many words they can read before a timer runs out. Note their score on the page so that they can try to beat it at a later date.

● The children can practise this in pairs, with one child pointing to words and the other reading.

Extension activities

● For further practice at reading the Phase Four and Phase Five tricky words, use the *Chimney* or *Maze* games.

● Put *Tricky word bookmarks* (▭) into reading books for practice at school and home.

3   Reading words with Phase Five graphemes

The children may still need to practise **blending** and reading words with the graphemes introduced in Phase Five Book 1. They must remember to say the grapheme sounds rather than the letter sounds. Revise this at the start of Phase Five Book 2 before introducing alternative pronunciations of graphemes.

· ·

You will need: *word cards* with Phase Five graphemes (▭).

· ·

Introductory activities

● Display the word cards in a list. Point to the first word, asking the children to sound and say it. Repeat with the remaining words, encouraging quick sounding and blending. Make sure that the children recognise the Phase Five graphemes and say the correct sounds when sounding and blending.

● If the children have difficulty with this, go through the words, identifying the two-letter graphemes and drawing **sound buttons** under the letters.

● If the children are confident with this activity, make it into a game, perhaps saying a child's name as you point to the word.

Sound Phonics activities (page 7)

● The children draw in sound buttons, then blend and read the words, before matching them to the pictures. Children who are confident with identifying graphemes and blending could do this without drawing sound buttons.

Extension activities

● Give the children a selection of Phase Five word cards. In pairs, play *Against the Clock* (see page 15 of this Guide) to encourage quick recognition and blending of words.

4   Spelling: counting phonemes

The children should continue to practise spelling words by **segmenting** and counting sounds, then choosing the graphemes to represent them. Revise this at the start of Phase Five Book 2.

You will need: *phoneme frames (▭); Phase Five sound mat (▭); word cards (▭).*

Introductory activities

- Display the phoneme frames and say a word, for example, *bird*. Ask the children to sound talk it with a partner, counting the number of **phonemes**, for example, *b-ir-d* (three phonemes).

- Decide on the phoneme frame needed for that word and write the graphemes on the phoneme frame, consulting the *sound mat*. Ask the children to repeat the process and to write the word.

- Repeat with other words containing different numbers of phonemes, such as *tie* (two) and *proud* (four).

Sound Phonics activities (page 8)

- The children sound talk, count the phonemes and write the words in the correct box. If necessary, encourage them to use the *Phase Five sound mat* to help them to recall graphemes.

- Some of the children may still find it helpful to make the words on phoneme frames using *phoneme frame letters* from earlier Phases (▭) before writing them.

---

*Note: if the children are familiar with forming the letters correctly, they can write directly onto the **phoneme frame**. Model the process, referring to the **phoneme frame letters** as you write each grapheme.*

Extension activities

- Word cards that have previously been used for reading activities can now be used for additional practice at segmenting to spell words. Include words with alternative pronunciations as they are introduced.

- Encourage the children to apply their segmenting for spelling skills whenever they are writing. For further practice, use word cards in games such as *Guess my word* (page 50 of this Guide).

5   Reading and spelling words with two parts

You will need: *word cards (▭); Phase Five sound mat (▭); small whiteboards or paper.*

Introductory activities

- Write a two-part word on the board, for example, *whisper*. Ask the children how they would read this word. Sound and blend the first **syllable** (*wh-i-s*), and then the second syllable, (*p-er*). Say the word (*whisper*).

- Remind the children that spelling is the reverse process. Say the sounds in the first syllable and write **wh-i-s**. Say the sounds in the second syllable and write **p-er**. Read the completed word. Ask the children to say the sounds and then write the word on their whiteboards or paper.

- Repeat with other two-part words.

Sound Phonics activities (pages 9, 10)

● The children read and match words to pictures (page 9) or write in the missing syllable to spell words (page 10). They could then challenge one another to spell words from both pages.

● If necessary, help the children by putting a slash between the syllables in the words on page 9. Use the *Phase Five sound mat* to support the children as they spell the words on page 10.

Extension activities

● In pairs, one child should pick up a word card and read the word to his or her partner, who checks it and says the word in a sentence. Both children should then cover the word, say the syllables and write the graphemes.

6　Reading questions with tricky words

Sixteen more tricky words are introduced in Phase Five Book 2. Some of these are introduced in the context of reading sentences or questions and others are introduced through reading stories.

. . . .

You will need: *reading question with the tricky word* (▭); *words to swap* (▭); *voting paddles* (▭).

. . . .

Introductory activities

● Display or write the question on the board.

● Read the question, pointing to each word. Ask the children to sound talk an unfamiliar but decodable word, for example, *Would you eat **s-p-r-ou-t-s** sprouts – Would you eat sprouts?* The children should answer with a show of hands or with *voting paddles*.

● Point to the new tricky word in the sentence and read it again. Write the word on the board and sound talk it, pointing to the graphemes. Discuss the tricky bit, where the letters do not represent the expected sound. For example, **oul** in *would* is not the expected spelling of the **u** sound.

● Ask the children to read the word a few times in and out of the sentence.

● Read the complete question again then change one word, for example, *Would you eat crusts?* or *Should you eat sprouts?* Ask the children to read this new question with a partner and to show their answers as before. Read the question together and compare answers.

● Discuss helpful patterns in tricky words, for example, *would*, *could*, *should* or *any*, *many*. *Who* could also be linked to *what* and *where*.

Sound Phonics activities (pages 11, 21, 30, 40)

● The children practise reading the tricky words and then read questions, selecting the correct answer. Once the activity is complete, the children should read the questions with a partner and compare their answers.

Extension activities

● Cut up the question and give a copy to each child, along with the *words to swap*. Ask them to change a word to make a new question, and then read it with a partner to decide whether it is a sensible or silly question. The children should see how many questions they can make.

● Incorporate the new tricky words in the classroom activities, for example, *How many ...?* in maths activities or *Who would/could/should ...?* in questions about stories. Look for the tricky words in shared and guided reading so that the children learn to recognise them automatically.

7   Alternative pronunciations of graphemes

In Phase Five Book 2, the children learn alternative pronunciations for some familiar graphemes.

· ·

You will need: *word cards with alternative pronunciations of the grapheme (📖).*

· ·

Introductory activities

● Display a word where the grapheme represents the more familiar sound, for example, **o** in *shock*. Ask the children to sound and read the word (**sh-o-ck** *shock*), then say it in a sentence.

● Display a word with the alternative pronunciation, such as *most*. Sound talk and read it using the incorrect pronunciation. Ask the children if the word sounds right and see if they correct you.

● In a different colour, write over the letter with the alternative pronunciation. Explain that in some words the letter is pronounced differently. Sound the word again, with the correct pronunciation, and then say it in a sentence.

● Display another word. Ask the children to sound talk it with a partner and to decide which pronunciation is correct. The children should try the alternative pronunciation if the usual pronunciation sounds wrong. Ask the children to say the words in a sentence. Repeat with another word.

---

*Note: some graphemes have two alternative pronunciations (**y, a, ch, ou**). For these graphemes, display enough words to illustrate all pronunciations.*

Sound Phonics activities (pages 12–15, 18–20, 24–28, 33–34, 36–38)

● The children sound and read words, and identify any with alternative pronunciations. Once the activity is complete, they should reread the words with a partner and say each word in a sentence to check that they both understand the word meanings.

● At this stage, many children will become familiar with words quickly and should not need to sound talk them more than once or twice.

● Some children may have difficulty recognising a word out of context. Try saying the alternative pronunciations in context, for example, *Is it a hu-man being or hyoo-man being?*

● Use the *Odd one out* activities on pages 20, 28 and 38 of the **Sound Phonics** activity book to revise alternative pronunciations of graphemes already covered. The children should identify the words with alternative pronunciations.

Extension activities

● Use the word cards for more practice at reading words with alternative pronunciations. In pairs, the children can read the words and sort them according to their sound. The words can either be posted into a *Tog posting box* (📖) or written on a *word sort* sheet (📖).

● The children could create their own 'odd one out' activities, to swap with or present to a partner. Each child selects four words with the usual pronunciation of the grapheme and one word with a different pronunciation. The children can use the word cards and the pupil book to compile their selection.

8   Reading sentences with alternative pronunciations of graphemes

You will need: *reading sentence with alternative pronunciations of a grapheme* (📖).

Introductory activities

● Display the sentence, for example, *Tog is a robot not a human being.* Read it together. Deliberately use the wrong pronunciation of a grapheme to sound and blend one word, for example, *human*. Look puzzled and see if the children correct the word.

● Demonstrate trying the alternative pronunciation, then sound and read the word correctly. Ask the children to read the complete sentence with you.

● Ask them to find other words in the sentence that feature alternative pronunciations of graphemes, for example, *robot*.

Sound Phonics activities (pages 16, 29, 39)

● The children read the sentences and select the answer or missing word. They should then read the sentences with a partner, checking that they have read the sentences correctly and chosen the correct answer.

● Support the children where necessary by reminding them of the alternative pronunciations of graphemes.

Extension activities

● Use words with alternative pronunciation of graphemes in captions on displays, for example, *The giant had a magic harp,* or on signs around the classroom, such as *Group 1, Music time*.

9   Writing sentences with tricky words

You will need: *writing sentence with the tricky word* (📖); *small whiteboards or paper; Tricky word mat three* (📖).

Introductory activities

● Write the tricky word on the board, for example, *so, little* or *what*. Ask the children to read it and say it together in a sentence or question.

● Sound talk the word, pointing to each grapheme as you say the sounds. Discuss the tricky part(s), for example, the double **t** and the **ul** sound at the end of *little*. Write over these in a different colour. If appropriate, relate this to other words with similar patterns, for example, *so* may be linked to *no* and *go*.

● Ask the children to trace ('finger write') the word on the carpet or table in front of them as they say the sounds. After they have done this a few times, rub the word off the board and ask the children to write it on their whiteboards or on paper. Check the spellings.

● Repeat the sentence or question from earlier. Ask the children to say it a few times. Then ask them to say one word at a time as they write it. Remind the children about spaces between words as well as the punctuation used in a sentence or question. Model this on the board if necessary.

Sound Phonics activities (pages 17, 22, 35)

● The children should practise spelling and using words to complete sentences, captions or questions.

Extension activities

● For additional practice, give the children a tricky word sentence to practise reading, saying, holding in their heads and writing.

● Confident children can write their own sentences, captions or questions using the tricky word. They could also use the tricky word in simple *caption books* (📖), for example, 'Big and little things'– *a big tree, a little bee*.

● Once the spelling of a tricky word has been introduced, expect the children to use the correct spelling whenever they write. Plan opportunities for the children to use the word in all subject areas. This could include using *what, when* or *why* to write questions in another subject, or *little* in story titles, such as *the little yellow bird*.

● Display tricky words and give the children a copy of *Tricky word mat three* to check the spellings. Gradually the children will retain the correct spelling without this support.

10   Homographs

Homographs are words that look the same but have different pronunciations and meanings. When reading homographs, the context of the sentence tells you how to pronounce the word.

· ·

You will need: *reading sentences* with homographs (📖); *word cards* with homographs (📖).

· ·

Introductory activities

● Display the first sentence, *The wind blew*. Read it together, sound talking the word *wind*.

● Display the second sentence, *Wind up the yoyo*. Read it, deliberately using the incorrect pronunciation of *wind*. Ask the children if it makes sense and see if they correct you.

● Demonstrate sound talking the word with the alternative pronunciation of the **i** grapheme. Read the sentence correctly. Check that the children understand the meaning of the word *wind* in this context.

● Explain that when two words look exactly the same, the context of the sentence can help you to work out the correct pronunciation. Discuss this with the children.

Sound Phonics activities (page 32)

● Working with a partner, the children should use the context of the sentence to work out the correct pronunciation of words. The children can check with a different partner to see if they agree on pronunciation.

Extension activities

● Give a selection of word cards featuring homographs to the children. In pairs, they should work out the two possible pronunciations of each word and put them into sentences. The children can then form groups of four to check their pronunciation of words and compare sentences.

11   Reading a story with tricky words

The remaining tricky words are introduced in the context of reading longer pieces of text: two stories and a description. These texts provide the children with a good opportunity to read a complete text using their phonic skills.

At this stage, the children should recognise many words instantly and should usually sound and blend unfamiliar words quickly. The challenge in these texts is provided through alternative pronunciation of graphemes, for example, *field*, *huge* and *cosy*, as well as the new tricky words.

You will need: *story sentence with the new tricky words (📖).*

Introductory activities

● Display or write the story sentence on the board.

● Read the sentence, pointing to each word. Ask the children to sound talk one or two unfamiliar but decodable words, for example, **m-o-n** *mon,* **s-t-er** *ster, monster*. Read the complete sentence together.

● Point to one of the new tricky words in the sentence and read it again.

● Write the word on the board. Sound talk it (if possible) and discuss the tricky bit. Ask the children to read and say the word a few times both in and out of the sentence. Repeat with the other new tricky words.

● Read the complete sentence again. Explain to the children that they will soon read about the characters mentioned in the sentence. Ask: *What do you know about the characters? I wonder what the story will be about?*

- Explain to the children that when reading the story or description there will be many words they recognise, but some words that they will need to sound and blend. Remind them that they might need to try an alternative pronunciation.

Sound Phonics activities (pages 41–43)

- Some of the children will be able to read the text independently or with a partner. Reading with a partner will encourage the children to check the accuracy and sense of what they read. Other children will benefit from reading the text in a guided group or one-to-one situation, where you can prompt and support them.

- Before beginning, remind the children to look for the new tricky words in the text. See if they can spot them. As the children read the text, prompt them to try alternative pronunciations of graphemes to read some words.

- If a child struggles with reading the text, share the reading with him or her. You could read the opening paragraph to the child and then ask him or her to take over for a few sentences or for the next paragraph, depending on how fluent the reading is.

- After reading the text, ask questions to check the children's understanding. These could be, *Was the grasshopper laughing at the end of story? Why/ why not? Do you think people liked the monster? Why/why not? Did Town Mouse enjoy his visit? Why/why not?*

Extension activities

- Ask the children to reread the text, either silently or aloud to a partner or adult. This will help them to become familiar with more words and to build fluency and confidence.

- Set activities that involve responding to the story. The children could draw the characters or setting, or they could make a *caption book* (📖) to show the key events of the story. Alternatively, the children could think of questions to ask one another about the story.

- Provide opportunities for the children to apply their phonic skills and knowledge of tricky words to read a variety of texts in guided reading and across the curriculum.

Sound Phonics Phase Five Book 3

1 Revising graphemes

2 Alternative spellings: consonants

3 Alternative spellings: vowels

4 Writing sentences with tricky words

Phase Five Book 3 focuses on alternative spellings of **phonemes** and on choosing the appropriate **grapheme** for each word. Many of the graphemes are familiar from reading and some children will automatically apply this to their spelling. However, others will need a more focused approach to learning word-specific spellings.

1 Revising graphemes

Continue the 'little and often' practice of recognition and recall of graphemes. This should include the different pronunciations of graphemes introduced in Phase Five Book 2 and the alternative ways of spelling phonemes.

You will need: *small whiteboards or paper; the Treasure trail game (▭); counters.*

Introductory activities

● Use the suggestions on page 31 of this Guide to consolidate the children's understanding of graphemes introduced so far. To increase the level of difficulty, adapt the activities as described below to include different pronunciations of graphemes and alternative spellings of sounds.

Grapheme recognition:

● Say a child's name as you write a grapheme on the board and ask the child to say the sound. Encourage immediate recall and response.

● If there is an alternative pronunciation, ask another child to give the other possible sound before moving on to the next grapheme.

Grapheme recall:

● Say a sound and ask the children to write the grapheme on a small whiteboard or on paper.

● If there is alternative spelling for the sound, ask them to write another possible spelling until the main ways of representing the sound have been covered, for example, **ay, ai, a-e**.

Sound Phonics activities (pages 4, 20, 33, 42)

● For pages 4 and 20, point to graphemes and ask the children to say the sound or sounds. The children could practise this in pairs, with one child taking the role of the adult.

● On pages 33 and 42, the children should write the alternative spelling of vowel phonemes. They can then check their answers with a partner.

● Use the *Phase Three* and *Phase Five sound mats* (▭) to support recognition and recall of graphemes if needed.

Extension activities

● Use the *Treasure trail* game to practise Phase Five graphemes.

2 Alternative spellings: consonants

Phase Five Book 3 introduces the children to alternative spellings of some consonant phonemes. Common words with alternative spellings are introduced, along with guidelines for their use.

. . . .

You will need: *word cards* (□); *enlarged phoneme spotting sentence* (□); *small whiteboards or paper.*

. . . .

Introductory activities

Word sort:

● Tell the children the sound they will be focusing on, for example, **mm**.

● Say a word with the usual spelling of that sound, such as *mint*, and ask the children to **segment** and write it. Write the word on the board for the children to check. Repeat with other words, creating a list on the board.

● Say a word with the alternative spelling, such as *lamb*. Segment the sounds and write the word on the board, for example, *l-a-mb*. Ask the children to identify the grapheme for the target sound, in this case, the **mb** grapheme for the **mm** sound. Explain that this is an alternative spelling.

● Draw columns on the board for the two spellings. Display the word cards and ask the children to put them in the appropriate columns. Establish spelling patterns and guidelines to help the children choose the correct spelling (pages 91–94 of this Guide).

Phoneme spotting:

● Tell children the sound they will be focusing on, for example, **f**.

● Display an enlarged copy of the *phoneme spotting sentence*. Read it and ask the children to listen for the focus sound.

● Read the sentence again, pointing to each word. Ask the children to raise a hand each time they hear the focus phoneme. Underline the words containing that phoneme.

● Read the underlined words again and ask the children to identify which grapheme represents the focus sound. Write over the graphemes in a different colour.

● Look at the alternative spellings and establish patterns and guidelines to help the children choose the correct spelling (pages 91–94 of this Guide).

Sound Phonics activities (pages 5–12, 14–17)

● The children explore words with alternative spellings of a consonant sound or use the spelling guidelines to choose the correct grapheme for a particular consonant sound.

Note: pages 12 and 17 of Phase Five Book 3 revise spellings that have already been introduced to check the children's understanding.

Extension activities

- Expect the children to spell correctly all words introduced in Phase Five Book 3, and correct any words with misspelt phonemes. This provides a good opportunity to reinforce alternative spellings and to further develop word-specific knowledge. Draw attention to any words with the alternative spellings in subject-specific vocabulary.

> ### Games to practise alternative spellings
>
> *Grapheme sort:* give the children a set of word cards featuring alternative spellings of the focus phoneme. Ask them to sort the words according to their spelling and record them on a *word sort* sheet (▭) or on the appropriate *Phonic family tree* (▭). They can then practise segmenting and spelling each group of words.
>
> *Memory challenge:* challenge the children to remember and write five words that have a less common spelling of a grapheme, for example, **mb** for **mm**.

- The games on page 68 of this Guide may also be used for further practice.

3   Alternative spellings: vowels

Alternative spellings of long vowel sounds tend to be particularly problematic. The children must be aware of the alternative spellings of these sounds and should choose the correct form for each word. Developing word-specific knowledge of spellings continues in Phase Six and beyond.

· ·

You will need: *enlarged phoneme spotting sentence (▭); word cards with alternative spellings of the phoneme (▭); phonic family trees (▭); small whiteboards or paper.*

· ·

Introductory activities

Word sort:

- As with the consonants, tell the children which sound they will be focusing on, for example, **ear**.

- Display the word cards. Point to the first word and ask the children which grapheme represents the vowel sound, for example, **ear** in *year*. Write over the grapheme in a different colour.

- Ask the children to find other words with the same spelling of the grapheme. Move these words into a column headed **ear**.

- Ask the children to find a word with a different spelling of the phoneme, and write over it in a different colour. Identify other words with this spelling.

- Ask the children to suggest other words with the same sound and write them in the appropriate column, for example, *cheer* and *peer* or *near* and *dear*. If the children say a homophone, such as *dear* or *deer*, ask them to say the word in a sentence. This will help you to establish which word they mean before you write it on the board.

- Look at the columns of words. Establish spelling patterns and guidelines that will help the children to choose the correct spelling (pages 91–94 of this Guide).

Phoneme spotting:

- Tell the children the focus sound, for example, the long **a-e** sound.

- Display an enlarged copy of the *phoneme spotting sentence*. Read it and ask the children to listen for the focus phoneme.

- Read the sentence again, pointing to each word. Ask the children to raise their hands each time they hear the focus phoneme. Underline the words containing that phoneme.

- Read the underlined words again and ask the children to find the grapheme that represents the focus phoneme. Write over the graphemes in a different colour.

- Draw columns for each spelling of the grapheme, in this case, **ay**, **ai**, **a-e**. Write or stick the graphemes at the top of the columns and add the words identified in the sentence. Ask the children to suggest other words to go in each column.

- Discuss spelling patterns to help the children remember the correct spelling (pages 91–94 of this Guide).

Sound Phonics activities (pages 18–19, 21, 23, 25, 28, 31, 34, 36–41)

- The children read words and sentences, identifying the graphemes that represent the focus sound.

- They should then sort the words according to phoneme spelling, writing them in the appropriate columns.

Sound Phonics activities (pages 22, 24, 26, 29, 32)

- The children write words to go with the pictures, choosing the correct spelling of the phoneme. These are all words that the children should be familiar with. Encourage them to check their spellings if they are not sure.

Extension activities

Games to practise alternative spellings

Sentence challenge: the children should write a sentence that contains an example of each spelling of the focus phoneme.

Word challenge: write a particular spelling of a phoneme on the board, and ask the children to list as many words as they can remember with the spelling.

- The games on page 67 of this Guide may also be used for further practice.

Applying phonics to writing

Encourage the children to apply and extend their knowledge across the curriculum. Draw attention to alternative spellings of phonemes in subject-specific vocabulary, such as *gale*, *rain*, *hail*, *flake* in the weather, or *seed*, *bean*, *tree*, *heat* when growing things. Feature the words on displays in the classroom so that the children can check their spellings. Write the alternative spellings in different colours.

Use *phonic family trees* (▭) to help the children recall alternative spellings of vowel phonemes in independent writing. Display a large *Phonic family tree* in the classroom, writing an alternative spelling of the phoneme on each branch.

Independent writing

The children will still choose the wrong spelling for a phoneme in words they have not learnt to spell. This is normal at this stage, but correcting these misspellings allows you to reinforce the alternative spellings of phonemes and extends word-specific knowledge.

4 Writing sentences with tricky words

· ·

You will need: *small whiteboards or paper; a **sentence starter** with the tricky word* (▭).

· ·

Introductory activities

● Write the **tricky word** on the board, for example, *looked*. Ask the children to read it. Point to the word and say it in a sentence.

● **Sound talk** the word, pointing to each grapheme as you say the sounds. Discuss the tricky parts of the word, for example, **ed** pronounced **t** in *look**ed***. Write over the tricky part in a different colour.

● Ask the children to trace ('finger write') the word on the carpet or table in front of them as they say the sounds. After they have done this a few times, rub the word off the board and ask the children to write it on their whiteboards or paper. Check the spellings.

● Say the sentence again and ask the children to say it a few times before writing it. Remind the children about spaces between words as well as the capital letter and full stop needed in a sentence.

● Think of a similar sentence featuring the tricky word, for example, *The farmer looked hot,* and repeat.

● Introduce other words with similar patterns, such as *danc**ed***, *call**ed***, *ask**ed***. These all end with **ed** for past tense but **ed** sounds like **d** or **t**.

Sound Phonics activities (pages 13, 27, 30, 35)

● The children practise spelling the tricky words and using them to complete or to write sentences.

Extension activities

- More confident children can write their own sentences using the tricky word(s). Alternatively, the children could use them in simple *caption books* (▭), for example, *Some people can run fast, Some people can swim fast*.

- Give the children a *sentence starter* featuring the tricky word. Ask them to see how many complete sentences they can write from the starter.

- Once the spelling of a tricky word has been introduced, remind the children to spell it correctly whenever they are writing. Plan opportunities for the children to use the words in all subject areas. Words such as *looked*, *asked*, *called*, *Mr* and *Mrs* could all be used in story writing.

- When writing independently, the children can use a tricky word mat (▭) and classroom displays to check their spellings. Gradually they should become confident enough to spell these words without checking.

Sound Phonics Phase Six Book 1

1 Spelling choices

2 Spelling patterns

3 Reading and spelling tricky words

4 Spelling longer words

5 Reading a story

6 Adding **s** and **es** endings

7 Adding **ed** endings

8 Adding **ed**: spelling guidelines

9 Adding **ing** endings

Children starting Phase Six Book 1 should already know the sounds for common **graphemes**, including alternative pronunciations. Continue to reinforce graphemes to develop recognition of **digraphs** when reading words and develop recall of graphemes when spelling words.

Use the activities on pages 4, 5 and 18 of **Sound Phonics Phase Six Book 1** to check recognition and recall of graphemes.

1 Spelling choices

By the start of Phase Six Book 1, the children should know that spelling involves not only segmenting words into **phonemes** but also choosing the correct grapheme for those phonemes. In Phase Six Book 1, the children learn to be more accurate spellers. They learn word-specific spellings, as well as spelling guidelines which apply to a number of words. These include '**w special**' words (see page 72 of this Guide).

Spelling choice activities are included in Phase Six Book 1 to reinforce alternative spellings and to extend knowledge of word-specific spellings.

. . . .

You will need: *phonic family trees* (▭); *small whiteboards or paper.*

. . . .

Introductory activities

● Say the focus phoneme, for example, **ai**. Ask the children to write down the different ways to represent that sound and to hold up their answers. Write the spellings on a *Phonic family tree*, for example, **ai, ay, a-e**.

● Say a word containing the focus phoneme, such as *lake*. Discuss the possible spellings, for example, *layk, laik, lake*. Write these on the board and ask the children which one they think is correct. Encourage them to give reasons that relate to the guidelines and patterns introduced in Phase Five Book 3. These could include, 'not *layk* because the **ay** grapheme occurs at the end of words', or '*lake* looks right – it's like *cake, make, take*'.

● Ask the children to write a few words containing different spellings of the focus phoneme. If they are not sure of a word, encourage them to write it down and see if it looks right. Write the words on the corresponding branch of the *Phonic family tree* so that the children can check their spellings. Recap relevant guidelines or patterns from pages 91–94 of this Guide.

Sound Phonics activities (pages 7–9, 14–17, 21)

● *Long vowel sounds:* the children segment words and choose the correct spelling for the vowel sound. They then segment and spell words to go with the pictures.

● *Consonant choice:* the children choose the correct grapheme for each word. In later exercises they will be required to sort words according to spellings.

Extension activities

● Ask the children to collect and sort words with different spellings of the phoneme. The words can be written on a *word sort* (▭) or the correct branch of a *Phonic family tree* (either individual sheets or classroom display).

● Follow up in independent writing. The children should refer to their own lists and *phonic family trees* to make accurate spelling choices.

2   Spelling patterns

In Phase Six Book 1, the children are introduced to spelling guidelines that apply to groups of words, such as 'w special' words (see below), contractions and the **suffixes s**, **es**, **ing** and **ed**.

· ·

You will need: *introducing spelling guidelines sentence* (▭); *word cards* (▭); *grapheme cards* (▭) *or plastic letters* (▭).

· ·

Introductory activities

● Display the first sentence. Read it together, pointing to each word. Underline the first example of a 'w special' word, such as *wasp*, or a contraction, such as *don't*. Ask the children to spot the other word with the same spelling pattern and underline it. Repeat with the second sentence.

● Write the four underlined words on the board and discuss the following spelling guidelines.

> *'w special'*: an **o** sound after a **w** or **kw** sound is often spelt with the letter **a**. An **ur** sound after the letter **w** is often spelt **or**.
>
> *Shortened forms*: these occur when two words are run together. Discuss which two words are run together in each of the four examples. Use grapheme cards or plastic letters to demonstrate the apostrophe, for example, make do not and push the words together. Remove the **o** of *not* and replace it with an apostrophe. Explain that the apostrophe replaces the missing letter(s).

Sound Phonics activities (pages 10–11, 22–23)

● The children find other examples of words featuring the spelling guideline and practise reading words featuring previously taught graphemes.

● They practise reading and writing the shortened forms of words.

Extension activities

● Use the word cards for additional practice at spelling words that follow the guideline, for example, use a word sort sheet (▭) for 'w special' or play *Guess my word* (see page 50 of this Guide) for shortened forms.

● Search for more words that follow the spelling pattern or guidelines in the learning environment.

3 Reading and spelling tricky words

The children should already be aware that words are not always spelt as they sound. Many **high-frequency words** have tricky parts and the children need to develop a method for finding and remembering these.

You will need: *writing sentence with a tricky word* (▭).

Introductory activities

- Write one of the featured **tricky words** on the whiteboard, for example, *water*. Ask the children to **sound talk** the word as you draw the **sound buttons**. If the word has more than one **syllable**, sound talk each syllable in turn, for example, *a-n/i/m-a-l*.

- Ask the children to find the tricky bit of the word, such as the **a** spelling of the **or** sound in *water*. Write over it in a different colour. Suggest ways to remember the tricky part of the word, for example, say *w-at-er* as it is written. Ask the children to write the word a few times as they say it.

- Repeat with another word so that the children become familiar with the process.

Sound Phonics activities (pages 12–13, 34, 38)

- The children use this process to practise reading and spelling tricky words. They should then test one another.

- The children also invent and write sentences that include two tricky words to practise spelling words in context.

Extension activities

- Give the tricky word sentence to the children to read and remember. They should then turn over the sentence, write it down and check it.

- The children can also write their own tricky word sentences using two or three words from the exercises.

4 Spelling longer words

Introductory activity

You will need: *word cards with polysyllabic words* (▭); *Word sort two* (▭).

- Say some two-, three- or four-syllable words and ask the children to clap the syllables with you, for example, *fin/ish*, *Sat/ur/day*, *hel/i/cop/ter*. Make sure the children say and clap syllables, rather than the separate phonemes.

- Say a word, then clap and count the syllables as above. Draw a line on the board for each syllable. Ask the children to segment the sounds in each syllable and tell you the letters to write. Read the complete word.

- Repeat with another word. Help the children to use the same process to write the word. Clap and count the syllables, draw the lines, say each syllable in turn, then segment the sounds and write the letters.

Sound Phonics activities (pages 6, 19, 20)

- On page 6, the children segment and spell two-part words to match the pictures and identify those featuring one or two long vowel sounds.

- In the later activities, they should identify and count the syllables in **polysyllabic words,** such as *roundabout* and *alligator,* sorting words on page 19 and spelling words to go with pictures on page 20.

Extension activities

- For further practice at identifying syllables, give the set of word cards to the children. Ask them to sort the words according to the number of syllables and record them on *Word sort two.*

- For more confident spellers, give each pair or group a set of word cards. The children should take it in turns to pick up a card and read their word to the group. The others clap and count the syllables, draw the lines and write the letters. The word card is then revealed for the children to check spellings.

5   Reading a story

At the start of Phase Six, the children should be able to read common words automatically but use **segmenting** and **blending** for unfamiliar words. Sounding and blending will often be silent but it may occasionally help to do it aloud.

The children should start to read longer, less familiar texts with increasing accuracy and fluency. As they become confident at decoding words, the focus will move on to comprehension.

Two stories and an assessment piece are included in Phase Six Book 1 but it is assumed that children will now be reading a wide range of material in many different contexts. These texts are used to introduce spelling conventions, but they could first be used to focus on decoding or comprehension.

. . . .
You will need: *either story from Sound Phonics Phase Six Book 1.*
. . . .

Introductory activities

- Introduce the title. Some of the children may already be familiar with the story. Encourage predictions about the story.

- Recap the phonic skills and knowledge that the children need to work on, including specific graphemes, automatic recognition of high-frequency words and reading longer words.

Sound Phonics activities (pages 22, 28)

- Confident readers could read the story silently to themselves, focusing on comprehension, or they could read it aloud with a partner to focus on reading accurately and fluently.

- Others may benefit from reading the story in a guided group or one-to-one situation with an adult. The adult can support them in applying their phonic knowledge to read words and can ask questions to check comprehension.

- The children should reread the story, either silently or aloud with a partner. This will familiarise them with more words and develop their reading fluency.

Extension activities

● The children could make a *caption book* (▢) to show the key events of the story, or they could ask one another questions about the story.

6   Adding s and es endings

· ·

You will need: *word cards* with nouns or verbs (▢); *voting paddles* (▢) *with* s *and* es *on; Word sort one* (▢).

· ·

Introductory activities

● Say a word in singular form, such as *bone,* and ask the children to help you spell it. Say the plural, for example, *lots of bones*. Again ask the children how to spell it. Explain that the **s** is added if there is more than one.

● Say some singular words and ask the children to write the plural, for example, *hands*, *toes*, *ears*.

● Say the word *box*. Sound talk and write it, then say the plural. Sound talk it and write the plural word. Emphasise the **iz** sound and underline the **es** spelling. Explain that an extra **iz** syllable indicates that **es** is added rather than **s**.

● Say a word and ask the children to work out the plural with a partner. They should decide whether the plural needs **s** or **es** and then hold up a *voting paddle* to show their choice. Write the word on the board.

● Repeat with six more words, then look at the words on the board and discuss the spelling patterns. Where a word ends in **ch**, **sh**, **x** or **ss**, add **es**.

● On another occasion, try adding **s** or **es** to verbs rather than nouns.

Sound Phonics activities (pages 24–27)

● The children practise adding **s** or **es** to verbs and nouns. They should use their phonic knowledge to spell words and should recognise that when **es** is added, the word gains a syllable.

● Simple texts are used to introduce the children to adding **s** and **es** in context.

Extension activities

● Give to the children the set of word cards and label *Word sort one* with *add s* and *add es*. Ask them to go through the words, deciding whether **s** or **es** should be added, before writing the words on the correct postbox. Alternatively, the children can post the words into *Tog posting boxes* (▢) with the same labels.

● The children should apply the rule in independent writing across the curriculum. Provide writing activities that require the children to use plurals or verb forms ending with **s** or **es**. These could include lists of objects in stories (*In the chest I found ...*) or lists of objects required for an activity. The children could also write *caption books* (▢), or their own version of 'My little brother' (**Sound Phonics Phase Six Book 1**, page 27).

7   Adding ed endings

The **ed** suffix on past tense verbs can cause problems with spelling, as it often sounds like **d**, **t** or **id**. The children must understand the concept of a past tense before they spell words ending **ed**. In Phase Six Book 1 a story in the past tense is used to introduce this.

You will need: *an enlarged copy of 'The red balloon'* (📖); *word cards with verbs* (📖); *small whiteboards or paper.*

Introductory activities

● Display an enlarged copy of 'The red balloon' and read the story with the children.

● Ask the children to identify all the verbs ('doing' or 'action' words), for example, *What did the lady/dog/ducks do?* Underline every past tense verb in the passage. Discuss the common feature of these words (they all end in **ed**).

● Explain that the **ed** endings show that the events happened in the past. Change some verbs to the present tense to show the difference, for example, *a balloon floats away ... a lady points at it ...*

● Take down the story and read it aloud. Pause at each verb so that, in pairs, the children can write the word on their whiteboards or paper.

● Display the story again and ask the children to check their spellings. Focus on each word in turn, showing that the ending of past tense verbs is spelt **ed**, even though it can sound like **d** (*played*), **t** (*barked*) or **id** (*drifted*).

Sound Phonics activities (pages 28–33)

● The children look and listen for words ending **ed**, highlighting these in their activity book. They should also check and correct the spelling of words with different pronunciations of this ending.

● On pages 32–33, the children write captions and sentences in the simple past tense, applying their knowledge of **ed** endings to spell verbs.

Extension activities

● Use the word cards to reinforce the idea of past tense and **ed** endings. In pairs, one child picks a verb and says it in a sentence, for example, *Today I sail across the sea.* His or her partner responds by saying the sentence in the past tense, for example, *Yesterday, I sailed across the sea.* They then both write the past tense verb. This could also be done in small groups.

● Make sure that the children apply this rule in their own writing, for example, when writing postcards or the diary of a character from a story.

● Once the children are familiar with the regular past tense ending **ed**, they must learn the spelling rules for adding this ending to words.

8   Adding ed: spelling guidelines

You will need: *word cards that follow the spelling rule* (📖); *blank word cards* (📖); *Word sort one and two* (📖).

Introductory activities

- Display a word, such as *float*. Ask the children to say it in the past tense. Write the past tense word on a blank card and put it next to the word.

- Repeat with six words, using some that just add **ed** and others, such as *hated* and *tugged*, that illustrate the new spelling guidelines.

- Look at the words and point to a pair that 'drop the **e**' in the past tense. In a different colour, write over the **e** and **ed** on the base and past tense words respectively, for example, *like* and *liked*. Discuss the change. Ask the children to identify other pairs of words on the board that follow the same pattern.

- Once they have identified all examples, ask the children to describe the change. Summarise this in a simple spelling rule, for example, '*If the word ends with e, drop the e and add ed*'.

- Repeat with those words that follow the '*double the last letter*' rule. Explain that the last letter is doubled if there is a single consonant after a short vowel, for example, *hum* and *hummed*.

Sound Phonics activities (pages 35–37)

- The children should investigate and apply the rules for adding **ed**.

- To reinforce learning, the children can organise the words on *Word sort one*. Label the postboxes with the focus rules: *just add **ed*** and *drop the **e***; or *just add **ed*** and *double the last letter*.

Extension activities

- Give the children a selection of word cards featuring verbs and a copy of *Word sort two* labelled with the rules *just add **ed***, *drop the **e*** and *double the last letter*. In pairs, the children should read the word, decide which rule applies and write the past tense verb on the correct island.

- Make sure that the children apply these rules in their own writing, for example, when writing stories or recounts of events. Provide writing opportunities that require the children to use past tense verbs. These could include writing a poem following the pattern of *A walk in the park* (**Sound Phonics Phase Six Book 1**, page 37).

9 Adding ing endings

. . . .

You will need: *ing rhyme* (▭); *word cards with verbs* (▭); *Word sort one and two* (▭).

. . . .

Introductory activities

- Display and read together the *ing rhyme*. Ask the children to identify the verb in each line. Underline the verbs and explain that **ing** is added to verbs to say something is happening, for example, *playing*.

- Discuss other ideas for the poem. Display a word card, for example, *paint* or *slide*. Ask the children to use this verb to suggest a line for the poem, for example, *Sam is sliding* or *Priya is painting*. Write the correct spelling of the verb next to the word card.

- Repeat with six to eight words, some illustrating the rules being introduced, for example, *win* (*winning*), and others that just add **ing**.

- Look at the words on the board and point to a pair of words that follow a rule, for example, slid**e** and slid**ing** to illustrate the '*drop the e*' rule. Use a different colour to highlight the change in spelling. Discuss the change to the base word. Ask the children to identify another pair of words on the board that follow the same pattern.

- Once they have identified all examples, ask the children to suggest a spelling rule based on these words, for example, '*If the word ends with **e**, drop the **e** and add **ing**'.

- Repeat with words that follow the '*double the last letter*' rule. Explain that the last letter is doubled if there is a single consonant after a short vowel, for example, *jog* and *jogging*.

Sound Phonics activities (pages 39–43)

- The children should investigate and apply the rules for adding **ing** to words.

- For further reinforcement, the children can organise these words onto *Word sort one*. Label the boxes with the appropriate rules: *just add **ing*** and *drop the e*; or *just add **ing*** and *double the last letter*.

Extension activities

- Give the children a copy of *Word sort two* and the word cards featuring base verbs. Label the three islands, *just add **ing***, *drop the e* and *double the last letter*. In pairs, the children should go through the cards, deciding where each word belongs and then writing the **ing** words.

- Make sure that the children apply these rules in independent writing. Set writing tasks that provide opportunities to apply the rules, for example, writing their own version of 'The names ABC' (**Sound Phonics Phase Six Book 1**, page 42) using names of children in the class and different verbs.

Sound Phonics Phase Six Book 2

1 Reading and spelling two- and three-part words

2 Proofreading

3 Spelling choices

4 Reading longer texts

5 Adding **s**, **ies**, **ing** and **ed** endings

6 Learning to spell tricky words

7 Adding **y**, **ful**, **ly**, **er** and **est** endings

8 Adding the prefixes **un** and **dis**

The children should now recognise all common **graphemes** and their alternative pronunciations. Continue to reinforce and revise any graphemes that cause difficulty, particularly **digraphs** for long vowel **phonemes**. Use the activity on page 4 of **Sound Phonics Phase Six Book 2** to check recognition of graphemes, and record any that still require practice and reinforcement.

1   Reading and spelling two- and three-part words

· ·

You will need: *word cards with polysyllabic words* (▢▢).

· ·

Introductory activities

Reading:

● Display a two- or three-syllable word, for example, *ambulance*. Recap breaking words up into **syllables** to read them, for example, *am/bu/lance*.

● **Sound talk** and **blend** each syllable and then say the complete word. Demonstrate trying alternative pronunciation of graphemes if appropriate. Ask the children to repeat the process.

● Display three more words for the children to sound and blend. If the children recognise the word automatically there is no need to blend it.

Spelling:

● Say a two- or three-syllable word. Ask the children to clap and count the syllables. Draw a line for each syllable.

● Ask the children to **segment** the sounds in each syllable in turn and to tell you the letters to write. Discuss spelling choices if there are alternative spellings of phonemes.

● Repeat with another word. This time, support the children as they use the same technique to write the word. They should clap and count the syllables, then draw the lines and say each syllable. They should then segment the sounds and write the letters.

Sound Phonics activities (pages 5–6, 32)

● On page 5, the children are timed as they read two- and three-part words. They should be encouraged to sound and blend any unfamiliar words, including those with alternative pronunciations of graphemes.

● On pages 6 and 32, the children should segment and spell two- and three-part words to go with pictures. If children find this difficult, remind them to clap the syllables and segment each part separately.

● Once the exercise is complete, the children can challenge one another to read or spell words from the page.

Extension activities

● Give children the set of word cards with polysyllabic words to use in the game *Against the clock* (see page 15 of this Guide).

● The children should apply these skills when reading and writing independently. Contextual information will often help the children to pronounce **polysyllabic** words correctly when reading.

● In guided reading, pick out one or two longer words from the text to sound and blend prior to reading. This should help the children to read the words automatically in the text.

2   Proofreading

Introduce the children to **proofreading** to help them learn to check their own spelling of words.

. . . .

You will need: *introducing proofreading text (▭).*

. . . .

Introductory activities

● Display the text and read through it, with the children following. Explain that you want them to look for words where the spelling is phonically plausible but incorrect.

● Encourage the children to help you identify any words that look wrong. Discuss alternative spellings, referring to *phonic family trees (▭)* or other displays of words in the classroom.

Sound Phonics activities (page 7)

● In pairs, the children proofread the passage. They should identify and correct spelling mistakes, referring to displays and lists of words in the classroom to help them.

Extension activities

● Provide opportunities across the curriculum for the children to proofread their own writing.

3   Spelling choices

In Phase Six Book 2, the children continue to develop spelling strategies and to build their word-specific knowledge. This will help them to choose the correct grapheme in instances where there are several possibilities.

Spelling choice activities are included in Phase Six Book 2 to reinforce alternative spellings for some difficult long vowel sounds and to extend knowledge of word-specific spellings.

. . . .

You will need: *word cards with alternative spellings of the phoneme (▭); Phase Three and Five word cards (▭).*

. . . .

Introductory activities

● Display a word, read it aloud and underline the spelling of the vowel phoneme, for example, *burst*. Ask the children to think of other words that have the same spelling. Write these words under the first word.

- Display a word with a different spelling of the phoneme, such as *dirt*. Ask for other words that have this spelling and write them underneath. If the children suggest a word with a different spelling, start another column for the new spelling pattern or for unusual spellings.

- Continue to introduce words until all spelling patterns are covered (*burst*, *dirt*, *worm*, *early*, *kerb*).

Sound Phonics activities (pages 9, 14, 22, 25, 27)

- The children select and write the correct spelling of the vowel phoneme in a selection of familiar words. They then check their spellings with a partner.

- Page 25 should be used to revise the spelling of high-frequency words.

Extension activities

- Give the children a selection of word cards with the different spelling patterns. Ask them to sort the cards according to spelling.

- Words can be recorded on a *word sort,* such as *Word sort one* (▢) for **ow** and **ou** words, or on *phonic family trees* (▢) with a branch for each spelling (**aw**, **oor**, **or** and **ore**).

- Follow up in independent writing. Encourage the children to use their word sort sheets and displays of *phonic family trees* to help them to recall spelling patterns and to check that they make the correct choice.

4   Reading longer texts

In Phase Six, the children should start to read longer, less familiar texts with increasing accuracy. They should read many words automatically and segment and blend unfamiliar words efficiently. At this stage it is important to increase both pace and fluency. The children should also gain reading stamina as they attempt longer texts.

Two stories and an assessment piece are included in Phase Six Book 2 but it is assumed that the children will now be reading a wide range of reading material in many different contexts. This should include silent reading as well as reading aloud. As the children become confident at decoding words, the focus in guided and one-to-one reading will move to comprehension.

The two stories included in Phase Six Book 2 are used to introduce **prefixes** and **suffixes** but they can be read prior to this, focusing on decoding or comprehension if required.

• •
You will need: *either story from Sound Phonics Phase Six Book 2.*
• •

Introductory activities

- Introduce the title of the story. Encourage predictions about the story based on the title, for example, *Do you think these two characters will be friends? Do you know any stories about giants?*

- Pick out one or two words from the story to focus attention on applying phonic skills or knowledge, for example, words with rarer graphemes, longer words or words with suffixes. This should help the children to read these words automatically in the text.

Sound Phonics activities (pages 35, 40)

● Confident readers can read the story silently or aloud with a partner. They should focus on reading accurately and fluently and should monitor their own understanding of what they read.

● Children who need more support should read the story in a guided group, or one-to-one with an adult to prompt them. The adult should ask questions to check the children's comprehension.

● The children will benefit from rereading the story, either silently or aloud. This will help them to become familiar with more words and they will learn to read the story fluently, with appropriate phrasing and expression.

Extension activities

● Provide opportunities for the children to reflect on what they have read. They could write a *caption book* (📖) to show the key events of the story, using drawings to show how they imagine the characters, settings or events.

● Ask the children to write character descriptions, or to suggest thought bubbles for the characters at different points of the story.

● The children could ask one another questions about the story (including why and how questions), or they could write questions to ask the characters.

● Some children may enjoy retelling or acting out the story using role play, puppets or toys.

5   Adding s, ies, ing and ed endings

Phase Six Book 2 revisits the rules taught in Phase Six Book 1 for adding **ed**, **ing** and **s**, and introduces rules for words ending with **y**. The children will also learn conventions for adding other suffixes to words.

. . . .
You will need: *Word sort two or three* (📖); *word cards for adding suffixes* (📖); *voting paddles* (📖) *with the rules on.*
. . . .

Introductory activities

● Draw columns on the board. Write the known spelling guidelines (such as '*add s*' and '*add es*') at the top of the columns and recap the rules.

● Say a word or show a word card, for example, *pack* or *plant*. Ask the children to discuss with a partner which column the word belongs in. The children can use the *voting paddles* or a show of hands to indicate a column. Write the word in the correct column, with the suffix.

● Repeat with other words. Make sure that there are several examples in each column.

● Show a word ending in **y**, for example, *ferry* or *copy*. Write the word with the suffix added, for example, *ferries* or *copied*. Discuss how the word changes when the suffix is added. Start a new column for this word and add an appropriate heading, such as '*change y to i and add es or ed*'.

● Explain that the rule '*change y to i*' only applies to words ending with a consonant before **y**.

Sound Phonics activities (pages 10–13, 16–19, 21, 26)

- The children practise using known rules and explore the new rule. They use their knowledge of these rules to spell words. In later activities, the children practise using **ing** and **ed** in different contexts.

- Pages 10–13 focus on adding **s**, **es** and **ies**, using both writing and reading to consolidate the children's understanding of these suffixes. The children should think about the rules being applied and discuss this with an adult.

- On page 26 the children encounter irregular past tense verbs, where the **ed** ending is not appropriate.

Extension activities

- Provide the children with a further selection of word cards and a *word sort* sheet. Let them write the labels to indicate the rules for adding **e**, **es**, **ing** or **ed**. In pairs, the children pick a word card and decide which rule applies. They should then write it on the correct island *(Word sort two)* or in the correct sack *(Word sort three)*.

- Use the word cards for page 26 of the activity book. Ask the children to match the present tense verbs to the corresponding past tense form. Explain that these verbs are irregular in the past tense.

- Remind the children to apply the rules in independent writing. Provide writing opportunities for the children to focus on this, perhaps writing their own version of the poem 'Yesterday' (**Sound Phonics Phase Six Book 2**, page 17) or 'The number rhyme' (**Sound Phonics Phase Six Book 2**, page 13).

6 Learning to spell tricky words

In Phase Six Book 2, the children continue to develop methods for finding and learning difficult or unusual parts in **tricky words**.

. . . .

You will need: *Learning to spell sentence* (📖).

. . . .

Introductory activities

- Write one of the words to be learnt on the board, for example, *different*. Ask the children to say the word aloud and to clap and count the syllables. Draw a line under each syllable.

- Ask the children to say the phonemes in each syllable in turn. Discuss any distinctive features or tricky parts that need to be remembered, for example, *different* has the double **ff**, the middle **er** syllable and the **ent** ending. Write over these in a different colour.

- Discuss ways to remember these tricky parts, for example, write *dif/fer* and add *ent*. Ask the children to practise this a few times. Cover the word on the board and ask the children to write it. Reveal the word so that they can check each syllable.

- Repeat with another word so that the children become familiar with the process.

Sound Phonics activities (pages 8, 15, 20, 33–34, 36)

- The children use this process to learn how to spell a selection of words.

- They then work in pairs to test one another, perhaps taking it in turns to challenge a partner to spell a word from the page.

Extension activities

- Give the children the tricky word sentence to read and remember. They should turn the sentence over, then write and check it.

- The children can write their own tricky word sentence using two or three words from the page. They could then swap these or dictate them for another member of the group to write.

- Give the children more words to learn using the same technique. These could include more words related to the same theme, such as colour words, words they have misspelt in their writing or words related to a current topic.

7   Adding y, ful, ly, er and est endings

You will need: *word cards for adding suffixes* (▢); *introducing suffixes text* (▢); *Word sort two* (▢); *reading sentence* (▢); *words to swap* (▢).

Introductory activities

- Display the text and read it aloud. Underline a word with the suffix. Ask the children to identify the other word with the same suffix. Write over the suffix in a different colour, revealing the root word and the suffix. Discuss how the words are used, for example, *rainy* and *blowy* are used as describing words.

- Display a word and ask the children to orally add the same suffix. Write the suffix on the end of the word. Ask the children to say the word in a sentence. Repeat with two or three more words.

- For the suffixes **y**, **er** and **est**, repeat the activity with words ending in **e**, a single vowel and a single consonant. Discuss how the words change when the suffix is added (either dropping the **e** or doubling the last letter). The children should already be familiar with these changes from learning to add **ed** and **ing**.

---

*Note: no change is needed for **ful** and **ly**, even if the base word ends in **e** or a short vowel and single consonant.*

Sound Phonics activity (pages 23–24, 28–31, 40–43)

- The children practise identifying the suffix on words or adding the suffix to words. They then use the suffixed words in sentences.

- Once the activities are complete, the children can work in pairs to test one another on spelling the words.

● Make sure that the children understand the meaning of the words in these activities. Ask them to say a sentence using the word or to mime or act out the word. For those who find this difficult, say a sentence that makes the meaning clear and see if the child can give you another example.

Extension activities

● Provide the children with the set of word cards. Ask them to add the suffix to each word and use the new word in a sentence. For suffixes **y**, **er** and **est**, ask the children to sort the words according to the spelling change needed. They then can record these words on *Word sort two*.

● Cut up the introductory sentence and give a copy to each child. Ask them to create a new sentence by swapping the suffixed words.

● Ask the children to look for examples of words containing these suffixes when they are reading. Start a word collection area where 'found' words can be displayed, perhaps using sticky notes.

● Plan writing activities where the children can use words with these suffixes. These could include writing descriptions, comparisons or stories.

● In shared writing and at the start of guided writing, select one or two words with these suffixes for the children to spell.

8 Adding the prefixes un and dis

The children are taught about word structure and how prefixes such as **un** and **dis** are added to words.

You will need: *word cards for adding prefixes* (▢); *introducing prefixes text* (▢).

Introductory activities

● Display and read the text aloud. Underline a word with the prefix **un**, such as *unhappy*. Ask the children to identify the other word with the same prefix. Write over the prefix in a different colour to show the root word and the prefix. Discuss what the words mean and how the base word changes when the prefix is added.

● Underline a word with the prefix **dis**, for example, *disliked*, and repeat as above.

● Display a word card, such as *tidy*. Ask the children to orally add the prefix **un** or **dis**. Discuss what both words mean and ask the children to make a sentence using the word both with and without the prefix, for example, *The library is tidy but the cloakroom is very **un**tidy*.

● Write the word on the board and add the prefix. Establish that the spelling does not change when a prefix is added. Repeat with a few more words using both **un** and **dis** prefixes.

Sound Phonics activities (pages 35, 37–39)

● The children practise identifying and adding the prefixes **un** and **dis** to words. They then practise using the words in sentences on page 39.

● Once the activities are complete, the children can work in pairs to test one another on their spelling.

● Make sure that the children understand the meaning of the words. Ask them to say a sentence using the word, both with and without the prefix. Alternatively they could mime or act out the two words, for example, *well* and **un**well, *pack* and **un**pack.

● If necessary, support the children by saying a sentence that demonstrates the meaning of the word and then ask the children to give another example.

Extension activities

● Provide the children with the set of word cards. Ask them to add the prefix **un** or **dis** to make a new word and then use them to make up sentences.

● Plan writing activities where the children have the opportunity to use words with these prefixes, perhaps writing descriptions of contrasting characters, for example, *Cinderella was kind and **un**selfish but her sisters were **un**kind and very selfish*.

Assessment in Sound Phonics

Assessment is an on-going process and should be part of every phonics session. It includes observations during introductory activities, as well as evidence from both the **Sound Phonics** and extension activities. It also involves monitoring the application of phonic learning in everyday situations. Together, this information will indicate the children's level of understanding and highlight anything that should be revised. You will also be able to identify any specific problems that need to be resolved.

In addition to this on-going assessment, each **Sound Phonics** activity book ends with a set of assessment tasks and assessment statements. These help you to track each child's progress and identify any gaps or difficulties.

---

*Note: Sound Phonics Phase One does not contain assessment tasks or assessment statements. Instead, assessment is based on careful observation during activities. To help you focus these observations, 'Observe and record' advice is given in the **Teaching notes** for Phase One. For a full explanation, see page 1 of this Guide.*

In Phases Two to Five the main assessments are a **sound check**, **blending check**, **segmenting check** and **tricky word check**. In the Phase Six books there is a **reading assessment** and a **spelling assessment**.

When carrying out the assessment tasks:

● work with individual children (rather than groups), so that you can fully assess each child's abilities

● ensure that the assessments are not threatening

● do not attempt all the assessments in one session, as the children will struggle to concentrate for that amount of time

● use the record and analysis sheets (▢) to note each child's progress and to analyse errors.

Sound check

This task assesses the children's knowledge of letter–sound correspondences. Details of how to carry out the assessment are given on the activity page.

The child's responses can either be recorded directly on the page or on the *group record sheet* (▢). Although responses are recorded on a group sheet, it is important to carry out the assessment with individual children.

Tick the **graphemes** that the child sounds correctly, and note any incorrect responses on the record sheet, writing the exact response given. This can help to identify specific confusions, for example, confusing **d** and **b** (a visual confusion) or **d** and **t** (an auditory confusion).

Blending check

This task assesses the child's ability to recognise graphemes, say the sounds and then **blend** them to read words.

Sometimes this assessment involves blending made-up words. When you introduce the blending check, tell the child whether the words are real or made up. If it helps, introduce made-up words as 'words used by aliens', but ensure that the children understand the purpose of the activity. Use your professional judgement – intervene if you think a child is confused by the task or is trying to turn the made-up words into real words.

Point to each word in turn and ask the child to say the sounds, then the word. Record the child's response on the blending and segmenting *analysis sheet* (□).

Note: there is a response sheet for each **Sound Phonics** book and you will need a copy for every child.

Tick all words that are sounded and blended correctly but record any incorrect attempts in full, noting exactly what the child says. This should help you see where and why the errors occurred. For example, a child might be saying individual letters rather than recognising two-letter graphemes, such as *c-h-i-l-l* rather than *ch-i-l chill* or *j-o-i-l* rather than *j-oi-l joil*.

Segmenting check

This task assesses the children's ability to **segment** sounds and identify the graphemes needed to spell words.

Introduce the activity by explaining that you want the child to say the words in **sound talk**. With younger children you might give an example and explain by asking them to, *Say the word like Tog does*.

Point to each picture in turn and say the whole word. Ask the child to sound talk the word and then to write the letters for each sound. If the child still has difficulty writing letters, he or she could use plastic letters or *phoneme frame letters* (□), or even point to the letters for you to write.

Record the child's responses on the blending and segmenting *analysis sheet* (□). Tick all words that are segmented and written correctly but record any incorrect attempts fully, noting exactly what the child says or writes. This should show you where and why errors occur. For example, a child might sound talk the word correctly but have difficulty recalling the graphemes, or may represent long vowel sounds with just one letter, such as *coch* instead of *coach*.

Tricky word check

This task assesses the children's ability to read **tricky high-frequency words** automatically.

When you introduce the task, explain that if the children recognise a word immediately they do not need to sound and blend it.

Point to each word in turn and ask the child to read it. Record the child's response on the high-frequency and tricky word *group record sheet* (□). Tick the word if the child reads it automatically. If the child segments and blends the word, return to it at the end of the assessment and see if he or she reads it automatically.

Circle instances where the child cannot give a response, says the wrong word or has to segment and blend a second time. Make a note of incorrect responses, recording exactly what the child has said. This may help you to understand confusions, for example, the child may be guessing the word by its initial letters rather than looking at the complete word.

Letter formation check: Phase Three to Phase Five Book 1

This is an assessment of the child's ability to form letters correctly.

You could carry out this assessment with a small group rather than individuals but it is important to watch the children as they write the letters, rather than just looking at the finished shapes. Notice whether the children form letters the right way round and start from the top of each letter.

Record your observations on the *group letter formation record sheet* (☐). Tick the letters that are formed correctly and note those that the child has difficulty with. Look for patterns in errors, such as forming **o**, **a**, **g** in the wrong direction.

Reading assessment: Phase Six

This task assesses how well the children use and apply their phonic knowledge and skills to read a text accurately and fluently. The children should read many of the words automatically and sound and blend any unfamiliar words.

Read the first paragraph to the child to familiarise him or her with the story and the flow of fluent reading. You can segment and blend one or two words if you wish, demonstrating how to do this quickly and effectively, and rereading a sentence to maintain fluency if necessary.

Ask the child to take over the reading. Follow his or her reading and use the Phase Six reading *analysis sheet* (☐) to record any errors made. Record errors as indicated below.

Error	Record
Unsuccessful use of phonics	Note sounds made and the word said (if any)
Word misread with no phonic attempt	Note the word said by the child
The child has to be told the word	Mark as 'T' or 'told'
Word is missed out	Mark as 'O' or 'omitted'
Word incorrect but corrected by the child	Mark as 'SC' or 'self-correction' (not an error)

Note: if the child sounds and blends a word successfully, it is counted as read correctly. However, you may want to make a note in the comments box if the child blends a lot of words, slowing the pace and losing fluency and sense.

Stop the assessment if the child makes 10 to 12 errors before the end of the passage and read the rest of the story to the child. If the child managed to read the story but was not fluent, encourage him or her to read it again independently. This is not part of the assessment but it will help the child to become familiar with the words in the story and provide practice at reading fluently.

Spelling assessment: Phase Six

The Phase Six spelling assessment is made up of three parts:

1 **Write the word to go with the pictures** assesses the children's ability to spell words using segmenting

2 **Add the ending** assesses their knowledge of the rules for adding **suffixes**

3 **Reading and spelling check** assesses how well they can spell high-frequency tricky words.

Note: you should make sure that the child can read the words before assessing whether they can spell them.

You could carry out the spelling assessments with a group of children, but ensure that each child spells the words independently, rather than with the help of others.

The children will need a separate piece of paper on which to write the words in the third part of the assessment. Say each word in turn and ask the children to write it down.

Mark the spellings for all three parts of the assessment and record each child's results on the Phase Six spelling *analysis sheet* (▭). Tick each focus that the child achieves and record any inaccuracies.

Assessment statements

The notes you have made on the analysis sheets, together with your on-going observations, will help you to assess each child's progress.

Go through the *Assessment statements* at the back of the book, preferably with the child, and tick them if the evidence indicates that the child is secure in the knowledge or skill. Leave blank any that still need to be worked on and discuss these with the child.

Take note of any particular gaps or areas of weakness and decide how you will deal with them. For example, form small groups for focused teaching of a particular skill or piece of knowledge, or ensure that individuals have additional support when practising skills that they find difficult.

Spelling choices and guidelines

Consonant sounds

Sound	Grapheme	Spelling guidelines	Activity book
c (hard)	c	**c** is commonly used at the start of words, and is most likely to occur before **a, o, u**	Phase Five Book 3
	k	**k** is commonly used at the start of words, and is most likely to occur before **e, i, y** **k** also follows long vowel sounds or consonants at the end of words	
	ck	**ck** follows short vowel sounds at the end of short words	
	ch	**ch** occurs only in a few words (*school, chorus*)	
ch	ch	**ch** usually follows a long vowel sound or consonant	Phase Five Book 3
	tch	**tch** usually follows a short vowel sound at the end of words (although there are exceptions: *much, such, rich, which*)	
f	f	**f** is the usual grapheme for this sound	Phase Five Book 3
	ff	**ff** follows short vowel sounds at the end of short words	
	ph	**ph** is only used in a few words (not 'everyday words')	
j	j	**j** is the usual grapheme for the sound, but it is never used to represent this sound at the end of English words	Phase Five Book 3
	dge	**dge** is used immediately after a short vowel sound at the end of words	
	g	**g** is sometimes used before **e, i** and **y** (*gem, magic*)	
	ge	**ge** occurs after a long vowel sound or consonant at the end of words	
m	m	**m** is the usual grapheme for this sound	Phase Five Book 3
	mb	**mb** occurs at the end of a few words, which the children will need to learn	
n	n	**n** is the usual grapheme for this sound	Phase Five Book 3
	kn	**kn** occurs at the beginning of a few words, which the children will need to learn	
	gn	**gn** is rarer than **kn** and occurs at the beginning of a few words, which the children will need to learn	
		*Hundreds of years ago the **k** and **g** were sounded. This can be a useful way to help the children remember the spellings, for example, **k**-n it, **g**-n aw.*	
r	r	**r** is the usual grapheme for this sound	Phase Five Book 3
	wr	**wr** occurs at the start of a few words, which the children will need to learn	

Sound	Grapheme	Spelling guidelines	Activity book
s	c	**c** is often used before **e**, **i** and **y** (*c*ity)	Phase Five Book 3

Phase Six Book 1 |
	s	**s** is the usual grapheme for this sound	
	se/ce	**se/ce** usually follows a long vowel sound or consonant at the end of words	
	ss	**ss** usually follows a short vowel sound at the end of words	
	st	**st** occurs in the middle of a few words, which the children will need to learn	
v	v	**v** is the usual grapheme for this sound	Phase Five Book 3
	ve	**ve** is almost always used to represent this sound at the end of an English word	
w	w	**w** is the usual grapheme for this sound	Phase Five Book 3
	wh	**wh** only occurs at the beginning of words	

Vowel sounds

Sound	Grapheme	Spelling guidelines	Activity book
long a sound	ai	**ai** is usually used to represent this sound in the middle of words (**ai**n, **ai**)	Phase Five Book 3

Phase Six Book 1 |
| | a-e | **a-e** is also used to represent this sound in the middle of words (**a**t**e**, **a**k**e**, **a**m**e**, **a**v**e**) | |
| | ay | **ay** occurs only at the end of words | |
| long air sound | air | **air** is one of the most common spellings of this sound | Phase Five Book 3

Phase Six Book 2 |
	ear	**ear** occurs in a few common words, which the children will need to learn	
	are	**are** is another common spelling of this sound, and is used particularly in verbs	
short e sound	e	**e** is the usual grapheme for this sound	Phase Five Book 3
	ea	**ea** occurs in a few common words (*head*, *bread*, *ready*)	
long ear sound	ear	**ear** is one of the most common spellings of this sound	Phase Five Book 3

Phase Six Book 2 |
| | eer | **eer** is another common spelling of this sound | |

Sound	Grapheme	Spelling guidelines	Activity book
long **ee** sound	ee	**ee** is one of the most common spellings of the long **ee** sound, and occurs mostly in the middle and at the end of words (**ee**p, **ee**d, **ee**k, **ee**t, **ee**l)	Phase Five Book 3
	ea	**ea** is another common spelling of the long **ee** sound, and occurs mostly in the middle and at the end of words (**ea**ch, **ea**m, **ea**t, **ea**l)	
	eat/eet and *eel/eal* are equally common patterns, which the children will need to learn in specific words		
	ie	**ie** occurs only in the middle of words (*chief, field*)	Phase Five Book 3
	e-e	**e-e** occurs only in a few words (*these, eve, theme*)	Phase Six Book 1
long **ee** sound (at the end of words)	ee	**ee** is the usual spelling of this sound at the end of one-syllable words	Phase Five Book 3
	y	**y** is often used at the end of a word (*very, happy*)	
	ey	**ey** is sometimes used at the end of a word (*key, donkey*)	
long **i** sound	igh	**igh** is used at the end of a few words, which the children will need to learn; (it is also important for the children to learn the pattern **ight**)	Phase Five Book 3
	ie	**ie** is used at the end of a few words, which the children will need to learn	Phase Six Book 1
	i-e	**i-e** is the most common spelling of this sound in the middle of words	
	y	**y** usually represents this sound at the end of words (*cry, fly*)	
short **o** sound	o	**o** is the usual grapheme for this sound	Phase Five Book 3
	a	**a** often represents an **o** sound following **w** and **qu**	Phase Six Book 1
long **o** sound	oa	**oa** is one of the most common spellings of this sound in the middle of words	Phase Five Book 3
	oe	**oe** occurs at the end of a few words, which the children will need to learn	Phase Six Book 1
	o-e	**o-e** is one of the most common spellings of this sound in the middle of words	
	ow	**ow** is usually used to represent this sound at the end of words	

Sound	Grapheme	Spelling guidelines	Activity book
long **oo** sound	**oo**	**oo** is one of the most common spellings of this sound in the middle of words	Phase Five Book 3 Phase Six Book 1
	ue	**ue** often represents this sound at the end of a word	
	u-e	**u-e** is one of the most common spellings of this sound in the middle of words	
	ew	**ew** often represents this sound at the end of a word and sometimes elsewhere	
long **or** sound	**au**	**au** is an alternative spelling of this sound (**Au**gust, **au**thor)	Phase Five Book 3 Phase Six Book 2
	aw	**aw** is an alternative spelling of this sound (s**aw**, y**aw**n)	
	or	**or** is the usual spelling of this sound	
	our	**our** is used in some common words, which the children will need to learn (f**our**, y**our**)	
	a[l]	**al** is a common pattern, which the children will need to learn (c**al**l, f**al**l, t**al**k, ch**al**k)	
long **ow** sound	**ow**	**ow** is used to represent this sound at the end of words and elsewhere in words (n**ow**, **ow**l, t**ow**n)	Phase Five Book 3 Phase Six Book 2
	ou	**ou** is not found at the end of words; common patterns include -**ou**d, -**ou**t, -**ou**nd	
long **oy** sound	**oy**	**oy** occurs at the end of words	Phase Five Book 3
	oi	**oi** usually represents this sound in the middle of words	
long **ur** sound	**ur**	**ur** occurs in the middle and at the end of a word (ch**ur**ch, f**ur**)	Phase Five Book 3 Phase Six Book 2
	ir	**ir** occurs in the middle and at the end of a word (g**ir**l, s**ir**)	
	er	**er** occurs in the middle and at the end of a word (f**er**n, h**er**)	
	ear	**ear** is found only in the middle or at the start of a word (l**ear**n, **ear**th)	
	w(or)	**or** only occurs after the letter **w** (w**or**d, w**or**k, w**or**m)	

Glossary

adjacent consonants	two or three consonants next to one another in a word (*stop, west*).
alliteration	words in close proximity that begin with the same sound (*jolly Jack jumps*).
blend	merge the individual sounds together to make a word, for example, blend *c-u-p* to make *cup*.
CVC word	a word with three sounds in the order consonant (C) vowel (V) consonant (C) (*hat* or *hoot*).
CCVC, CVCC, CCVCC word	a word consisting of adjacent consonants and vowels in the order prescribed by the letters (see above) (*stop, west, twist*).
decodable words	words that can be read using current phonic knowledge.
digraph	two letters that together make one sound (**sh, ch** – consonant digraphs; **ai, ee** – vowel digraphs).
grapheme	a letter or sequence of letters representing one sound or phoneme.
homograph	a word that has the same spelling as another word but has a different pronunciation and meaning (*bow – a bow tie, take a bow*).
high-frequency words	the words most frequently encountered both in children's reading material and in their own writing.
phoneme	the single smallest sound within a word (*dog* has three phonemes, **d-o-g**).
polysyllabic words	words with more than one syllable or beat (*Sep/tem/ber* has three syllables).
prefix	a part that can be added to the start of a word to change its meaning (**un**/*happy*).
proofread	check a piece of writing for spelling errors.
segment	split a word up into its separate sounds in order to spell it, for example, split *cat* into **c-a-t**.
sound button	a dot or small circle put beneath a letter to help children sound and blend words: they touch the *sound button* as they say the sound.
sound talk	the process of saying in order the phonemes (sounds) in a word.
suffix	a part that can be added to the end of a word to change either the tense of a word (*walk*, *walk**ed***) or the class of a word (*colour*, *colour**ful***).
syllable	a beat of a word (*sis/ter* has two syllables).
tricky words	words with unusual or unfamiliar spellings.
trigraph	a grapheme where three letters make one sound (**igh, air, ear**).

Schofield & Sims Sound Phonics books

Activity Books

These carefully graded books provide practice in the phonic knowledge and skills introduced through teaching. The first book, a reusable stimulus book, is followed by nine one-per-child activity books for the Early Years Foundation Stage and Key Stage 1.

1. Sound Phonics Phase One	978 07217 1144 7
2. Sound Phonics Phase Two	978 07217 1145 4
3. Sound Phonics Phase Three Book 1	978 07217 1146 1
4. Sound Phonics Phase Three Book 2	978 07217 1147 8
5. Sound Phonics Phase Four	978 07217 1148 5
6. Sound Phonics Phase Five Book 1	978 07217 1149 2
7. Sound Phonics Phase Five Book 2	978 07217 1150 8
8. Sound Phonics Phase Five Book 3	978 07217 1151 5
9. Sound Phonics Phase Six Book 1	978 07217 1152 2
10. Sound Phonics Phase Six Book 2	978 07217 1153 9

Teacher's Guide

The **Teacher's Guide** helps you to introduce key phonic skills, use the activity books effectively and reinforce new knowledge. It also contains spelling guidelines and full details on carrying out assessments.

Sound Phonics Teacher's Guide   978 07217 1223 9

Teacher's Resource Book

A bank of photocopiable materials to support the teaching and learning described in the **Teacher's Guide**. Resources may be photocopied for individual and pair activities or enlarged for use in group and whole-class work.

Sound Phonics Teacher's Resource Book   978 07217 1224 6

Rhymes for Reading

A collection of decodable rhymes designed for use in Phases Two to Four and linked to common Early Years and Key Stage 1 themes. It provides a valuable opportunity for the children to apply their phonic knowledge from an early stage.

Sound Phonics Rhymes for Reading   978 07217 1240 6

Free downloads

Further resources are available as free downloads from the Schofield & Sims website (www.schofieldandsims.co.uk). These are updated as necessary to meet the requirements of the National Curriculum, and may be used in the activities described in the **Teacher's Guide** or for further practice.